9/16/04

Happy Birthday, Jeanie?

dressed
to
grill

Remembering
those great days
of 2 gals dressed to
grill "Chamberlain H.S.
Picnics? Whoop-las"
We had fun?

Thanks for the
memories
girl —
Love, Cindy

Cheers

dressed to grill

Savvy recipes

for girls who play with fire

by **K**aren **B**rooks, **D**iane **M**organ, and **R**eed **D**armon

Illustrations by **BETH ADAMS**

CHRONICLE BOOKS

SAN FRANCISCO

Library of Congress Cataloging-in-Publication Data
available.

ISBN 0-8118-3139-6

Printed in Singapore

Designed by Reed Darmon
Illustrations by Beth Adams
Photographs by Mittie Hellmich

Distributed in Canada by Raincoast Books
9050 Shaughnessy Street
Vancouver, BC V6P 6E5

10 9 8 7 6 5 4 3 2

Chronicle Books LLC
85 Second Street
San Francisco, California 94105

www.chroniclebooks.com

dedication

To Mom, the best girlfriend of all.
— KAREN BROOKS

To my fabulous daughter, Molly.
Don't ever lose the girlitude.
— DIANE MORGAN

To my sister, JoAnn,
queen of the cowgirls.
— REED DARMON

contents

8

INTRODUCTION

Hey, grillfriend

13

CHAPTER 1

The year of grilling dangerously:
Cool tools and hot techniques

22

CHAPTER 2

Spice girls: Marinades, rubs and pastes

33

CHAPTER 3

The light stuff: Grilling the low-fat way

44

CHAPTER 4

Body work: Showing off the best parts

51

CHAPTER 5

Dishes of desire: Le hot date

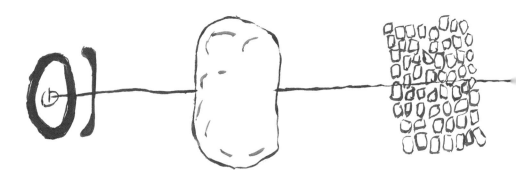

61

CHAPTER 6
Bonfire of the miseries:
Welcome back to bachelorettehood

71

CHAPTER 7
Sassy sides

80

CHAPTER 8
Desperately seeking sugar

90

CHAPTER 9
Liquid assets

98

PARTY PLANNER
Move over, Martha:
Entertaining
without stenciling your napkins

Notes/102
Index/106
Table of equivalents/107
Acknowledgments/108

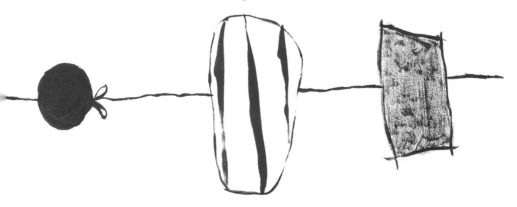

Hey, grillfriend

Let's face it. Right out of Eden's gate, we got the short end of the barbecue stick. Girls got the fertility ritual, complete with the backbreaking assignment of grubbing for roots, while men proved who really sits on top of the food chain by vying for the power of the flame pit. That whole scenario became carved in stone—men flushed with pride, bobbing and weaving above a carbonized hunk of hindquarter while women found solace in side dishes and nifty napkin folding. This guy-central arrangement has dominated the food furnace up through the Mesquite Grill Era as modern kings of the 'cue, decked out in urban aprons—mitt in one hand, lethal-looking tongs in the other— stage eight-hour rib marathons over culinary kilns. Rising up out of the smoke comes the essential image of our times: "I am da Man!"

To which we say, "So what?" In a world in which girls dunk and play hot hoops, orbit the earth, and slay vampires in their off time, the grill game's seating arrangement has changed. Females have rediscovered the fun of the flames.

We tasted it in childhood and lost sight of it in the process of becoming Hip Modern Women. Remember the first time we transformed a squishy little marshmallow into a hot, golden mass that exploded in our mouths like some magical fireball of smoke and sugar? Now, every summer, flickering coals unleash a cascade of smoky nostalgia: Girl Scouts, s'mores, and goofing around a bonfire; summer-camp secrets and soul-searching conversations carried deep into the dark, smoke-scented night. Today, from apartment rooftops armed with hibachis to high-design decks that double as social headquarters and grill heaven, women are fervently romancing the bone . . . and the food world will never be the same.

That's because men and women bring a completely different mindset to fire. For a guy, outdoor cooking is nothing less than a high-performance culinary rite. It's the raw and the cooked, Plato and the cave, honey and the ashes, the urge to hunch over something uncivilized but glorious. This is the inner ring of a guy's psyche, the one indestructible primordial link to his Neanderthal roots. The kick lies in the daylong immolation of tough, T. rex–sized meat—the whole spectacle writhing in a science-lab cauldron of chiles, chiles, and more chiles, plus samplings from whatever bottles have been lurking in the back of the fridge for the last two years. It's all about the long, slow burn, a secret sauce, prodding and poking, and sipping cold beer while pondering how to be a sensitive man in a barbaric world.

For girls, an all-day meditation is reserved for the more critical rituals in life, like going to a spa or figuring out how many calories you can burn hauling a 20-pound bag of briquettes from the store to the car to the deck, or watching martial arts tapes to bone up on the strategies for Nordstrom's half-yearly sale. Our grill theory is built on priorities, impulse, and creative adventure. It considers the unlimited possibilities for flavor, then ponders how to quickly sear the freshest ingredients over high heat with one goal in mind: instant pleasure.

Although we may not all be artists, girls tend to think of food as art. The grill is but a canvas where colors are explored, textures offer new challenges, and unexpected flavor combinations provide a tease or a taste of creative tension. Contrasting hues inspired You Goat, Girl (page 72), a still-life salad of grilled blue-black figs set against the grassy glow of steamed green beans and crumbly white goat cheese. Or consider Firm Thighs (page 47), which fuses Mexican *mole,* fiery flavor teasers, and grilled chicken into something new and outrageous, especially with a side of mashed potatoes. The secret is to get a frisky spice rub and a sensual sauce dancing thigh to thigh in a tango of lip-buzzing flavors.

But make no mistake: *Dressed to Grill* is not designer barbecue. It's not barbecue at all. It's grilling, through and through. We bring on big flavors, big spices, experimentation, and improvisation. Our recipes are leaner, more expressive, more exotic, and more open to interpretation than their primal-screaming, bone-suckin', dude food cousins. Meaning, they're in touch with the girl side of the grill. We love ingredients guys barely count as food: boneless, skinless chicken breasts; vegetables, and enough of them to qualify as a hanging garden in Babylon; figs, nectarines, and pears, all sizzling truly, deeply, madly on a hot grate.

When we control the heat, we don't worry about the grill of victory or the agony of the meat. We aren't competitive about sauces, and we hate to see a great one go to the grave unrecorded. We're into sharing. That's why every recipe in this book comes with its own "Cook and Tell," an inside tip on the joys and ecstasies of grilling.

For the aspiring grill girl who still doesn't know the difference between tongs and thongs, we're here to help. Check out "The Year of Grilling Dangerously," our handy-dandy, user-friendly guide to the art of grilling (pages 12–21). We've considered your manual-reading phobias and focus only on what you really need to know about a grill: How to buy it, light it, and accessorize it. The trick for singe-free hair? Black aprons—in or out? Not to worry. We've got those covered, too.

Dressed to Grill is pegged to the driving forces of a girl's life: romance and its opposite—dumped and out for revenge, bonding parties, everybody's-feeling-fat-and-on-a-diet dinners, sugar urges and splurges, plus cocktails and mocktails to satisfy the devil or angel within.

Our lab-tested recipes are simple and open to improvisation: We offer our treasured formulas but hope you'll play, experiment, and get inspired with your own personalized combinations. Think of these recipes as wardrobe basics to mix and match and build on. Directions include chitchat, sass, dissing on bad dates, hand holding on dishes you never learned from your mom, and calorie-burning exercises between cooking steps, even though you didn't ask for them. It's an ongoing dialogue, like cooking with a girlfriend at your side.

What we talk about is a smoldering fusion of a woman's instincts and the delicious flavors dancing on their edge. All this with the good sense not to take ourselves too seriously.

The soul of *Dressed to Grill* emerged from the crucible of countless flameouts. All the keepers here smack of our no-mistakin'-it brand of girlitude. For us, that translates to great food, great conversation, and great fun.

It's not just the boys' fire anymore. It's ours. It's yours.
— *Karen Brooks and Diane Morgan*

You grill, girl!

The year of grilling dangerously

1

Cool tools and hot techniques

GRILL DECISIONS
Our handy tips on buying
the big equipment

GRILL FASHIONS
An insider's guide to cool
tools and accessories

LIGHT YOUR FIRE
Grill techniques
demystified and
perfected

Grill decisions

Let's face it, girls: Buying a grill doesn't have the "glam" appeal of buying a new pair of shoes and choosing between sexy stilettos, primping pumps, or pedicure-demanding sandals. However, if you bone up on some facts, you can assume a command presence when walking into a patio shop, and we guarantee you'll feel that rush of empowerment. Yes! I'm a master of my own grill. A real backyard-grillin' handy ma'am. (Calm down—some assembly may be required.) Here's the scoop:

First, you have one major decision to make. Are you a charcoal-burning kind of gal or a flick-of-the-switch, gas-fired grill queen? Though purists would have you believe that charcoal rules, there is no right answer. If Alain Ducasse, the Michelin star–drenched chef, uses gas, so can you. Don't be bullied. Know thyself. If it makes you feel like a real woman to haul home 10-pound bags of briquettes and build a fire from scratch, think charcoal. But if 15 minutes, max, is your patience level for getting food on the grill, don't even think about it: Go gas.

Charcoal grills

The bottom line is flavor and price. Some grillmeisters swear by charcoal flavor, and they don't mind the time and fuss involved in starting a fire. Plus, charcoal grills are cheap. A kettle-style grill is nice, but if money is tight and you live in an apartment with only a balcony, you'll be amazed at what you can fire up on a hibachi or table-top grill. You don't need four burners to feel really hot.

We love kettle-style grills because of their versatility. Some models have a propane fire-starter for lighting the charcoal—totally cool if you're splurging. Look for a grill that has strong legs (why settle for anything less?), a hinged grate for easy access to the coals, a grate at the bottom for holding the charcoal, an ash catcher (don't try to say this too quickly to the salesman), air vents in the bottom, a lid for temperature control, side baskets to hold coals for indirect grilling, and a built-in thermometer. You'll even have a choice of colors: hot reds, cool blues, sleek blacks.

Gas grills

The word here is convenience. Assuming you have a full tank of propane, gas grills are ready when you need them. (Just like a guy— righhht!) It takes longer to put on lipstick than to turn on the flame, and after 15 minutes of preheating, you're good to grill. Gas grills have inverted V-shaped metal bars and lava stones or ceramic briquettes that create intense heat. As the sizzling juices and fat drip, smoke is created, flavoring the foods. Look for a sturdy, well-built grill with a heavy firebox; electronic ignition; separate heating zones (two is OK, three is good, four is going for the gold); heat controls for high, medium, and low; and a built-in thermometer. A gas gauge that shows when the tank is low is really helpful, but a backup tank (full!) is the sign of a smart grill girl. High-end grills have work spaces on either side—a most handy feature. Really fancy ones are equipped with a gas burner on the side for heating sauces or cooking corn. Grill colors are yours to decide.

Grill fashions

There are a few "must haves" for every grilling wardrobe:

Chimney starter

For charcoal grilling only. No nasty lighter fluid necessary. Just fill this large steel can (designed with vent holes in the bottom and a heatproof handle on the side) with crumpled newspaper and charcoal. Light a match to the paper, and let the coals begin to blaze. When they're hot, simply dump them in the grill.

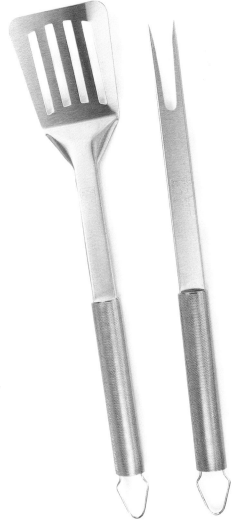

Tongs

Long, strong (preferably spring-loaded) tongs are essential for turning food and moving the coals around.

Spatulas

Long-handled metal spatulas are not negotiable. Buy oversized flexible ones with holes in them for easy flipping.

Grill fork

No stabbing, please. Just use for lifting. A long-handled one is best.

Basting brush

Buy two long-handled brushes with natural bristles (nylon will melt— you've been warned), one for oiling the grill rack and the other for slathering on sauces and glazes. Paintbrushes from hardware stores work, too; however, the handles are short, so be careful. Singeing the hairs on your arm isn't the best answer to hair removal.

Instant-read thermometer

A small-dial, thin-shaft, all-purpose tool used for measuring the tempera-

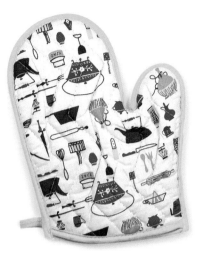

ture of everything. A must for expert grilling. It isn't meant to be left in the foods—you take a temp; get an instant read, as it were; and out it comes. Wash it before reinserting, or risk giving your guests food poisoning, which is not very tasty.

Grill brush

Like washing dishes and dusting, cleaning the grate every time you grill is one of life's necessary pains. Brass brushes with long handles last the longest.

Oven mitts

A pair of well-insulated, heavy-duty, long-down-the-arm oven mitts keeps your hands protected and your forearms shielded from unexpected flames. Yes,

you do look like a female escapee from the World Wrestling Federation. If you only have a short mitt, make sure it's thick—and hip.

Spray bottle or water pistol

Annie Oakley wouldn't be caught dead without a water pistol to tame those grill-fire flare-ups. Ride on over to your favorite hardware or toy store and arm yourself with a plastic spray bottle or hot pink water gun. Fill 'er up with water, and get ready to shoot.

Fly swatter

Who doesn't need some pest control? Take care of those tormenting dive-bombers with a good, old-fashioned fly swatter. We're partial to the ones with nice wooden handles for easy gripping and thin, flexible screening that zaps the buzzer before it knows what hit it.

Headbands

Keep those locks off your face and away from the flames. Split ends are hard enough to contain—you don't need burnt ends as well. Vanity rules here.

Aprons

Get creative while protecting your grill-party clothes. Scout vintage stores for those oddly spirited, perfect-mom prints or Modernist geometric patterns. Or, roam the racks at hipster boutiques. Pick something to suit the food and the mood: sexy, sweet, chic, or spunky. Black aprons, like black dresses, are always in fashion.

Lights and candles

Light up the night with a string or two of line lights. Check out some red, blazing chile-pepper lights; tacky alien heads; or a line of con-tempo, glowing white pods. Set the mood, and don't forget candles. Citronella votives get rid of the bugs, but big, fat, handmade Mexican candles may leave you burning with desire.

Light your fire

You don't need a guy to light your fire. All you need are some facts on fuel, directions for starting the flames, and the methodology for direct and indirect grilling, plus a few pointers on getting your chips to smoke. Here goes.

Fuel rules

As far as charcoal goes, three choices are available. Lump hardwood charcoal (our fave) is also called "charwood" or "chunk charwood charcoal." This fuel is pure charcoal through and through, irregularly shaped, and free of impurities. It burns hotter and longer—just like a great date. You won't find it in convenience stores, but check out well-stocked supermarkets and specialty shops carrying grill gear.

Pillow-shaped natural briquettes are chemical free and made from pulverized charwood—a good choice if you can't find the lump stuff.

Composition briquettes are your ordinary, available-everywhere type of charcoal. The downside to this fuel is that it's not all charcoal. Manufacturers throw in sawdust, scrap lumber, paraffin, or petroleum binders and, in some cases, chemical additives to make it light more easily. If you're going to put chemicals into your pores or into the atmosphere, make it count: Dye your hair a fabu new shade or go on a jaunt to the beach with your best pals in a convertible sports car for an unforgettable weekend.

Light it up

Open the vents on the bottom of the grill. Use a chimney starter (pictured above) and follow the manufacturer's directions. When the coals are covered with a gray ash, spread them evenly over the charcoal grate for the direct-grilling method, or mound them to one or both sides of the charcoal grate for the indirect-grilling method. (Hang in there; we are about to explain all that.) It takes about 45 minutes for the coals to get hot enough for grilling, leaving you plenty of time to preen, polish, and greet your guests.

Hot, hotter, hottest?

Judging the heat level of a fire takes practice (like some other things); here's our less-than-scientific, but nonetheless reliable method. Think back to the days of playing hide-and-seek and counting "one thousand one, one thousand two . . ." It's the same idea here, except this time, you're not covering your eyes. Hold your hand 5 or 6 inches above the cooking grate and count off seconds—"one thousand one, one thousand two, one thousand three," and so on. If you're really feeling the heat and your hand is uncomfortable after 1 or 2 seconds, the fire is hot. If you can count 3 or 4 seconds, the fire is medium. If you can count 5 or 6 seconds, you have a low fire.

Direct grilling

This method is used for grilled foods that do not need long, slow cooking, such as burgers, veggies, fish fillets, and kebabs. As the name implies, you're grilling directly over the coals or burners. The coals are positioned directly below the cooking grate.

Indirect grilling

This technique is used for foods that need long, slow cooking, such as whole chickens, barbecued ribs, and whole fish. With indirect cooking you are, in essence, "grill roasting," because the grill is covered during the entire time the food is cooked.

For a charcoal grill, light the coals, and when they are blazing red, mound them against one or both sides of the grill (the choice will depend on the type and design of your unit). Some charcoal grills have special metal baskets positioned inside to hold the fuel in the correct position for indirect cooking. Place a drip pan—a disposable aluminum rectangular or round pan—directly below the food to prevent grease flare-ups. Position the food to be grilled on the opposite side from the coals or between the mounds of coals. Cover the grill and follow the recipe directions.

For a gas grill, light all the burners to preheat the grill. Once preheated, turn off the burners directly below where the food is to be cooked. Place a drip pan directly below the food to prevent grease flare-ups.

Where there's smoke there's flavor

Most of the punch from grilling comes when food juices drip onto the coals, producing smoke. If you desire extra smokiness, add some hardwood chips to the fire. Here's how: Buy yourself a bag of hickory, cherry, oak, or mesquite chips—or choose another flavor to play with. Soak a couple of handfuls in a bowl of cold water to cover for about 1 hour. This prevents the chips from burning; they just smolder. (You know that feeling.) Drain before using.

For a charcoal grill, throw some chips directly on the coals when you start to grill, and then add more later. Another method is to make an aluminum foil pouch. Fold a long sheet of foil in half. Place a big handful of prepared chips inside. Seal the edges on three sides by scrunching them together. Poke a few holes through the foil, and lay the pouch directly on the coals.

For a gas grill, use the aluminum pouch method, or throw a handful of prepared chips in an aluminum pie plate with a few holes poked in the bottom. If your gas grill has a smoker box, place all the prepared chips in the box and let the smoke billow.

The grate cleanup

A happy grill is one that is well maintained. (Aren't we all?) Clean the grate with a grill brush once you have preheated the grill. The burnt bits of food from your last grilling escapade loosen more easily when the grate is very hot. Pour some vegetable oil in a small bowl and use a long-handled brush to generously oil the grate just before you grill the food to prevent food from sticking. If you think about it (Martha would), clean the grate again after you finishing grilling.

Spice girls

Empower your food. Make it twist, shout, jump, dance, and sing. The key is to vary the rhythm and the method. Some moods call up a back-beat of fiery heat, others play to a laid back, patio-party tone. Females of the flame have rubs and pastes to suit the occasion, from Jerk Paste (page 30), designed for the 12-bite recovery heal-and-stab-a-thons after Mr. Wonderful disappears, to Mod Bods Mustard Marinade (page 25),

fennel

coriander

cayenn

MARINADES

Lemonology: A theory of vital ingredients

Mod bods mustard marinade

Hidden pleasures hoisin-ginger glaze

Forbidden nights Moroccan pesto

RUBS AND PASTES

Hot girls spice rub

Burning desire: An Indonesian blend

Jerk paste

Sisters of the revenge Indian spice rub

2

for a wickedly sensual grill fest. And no repertoire is complete without the secret success of Lemonology (page 24), where, in almost any situation, lemon, garlic, and rosemary hit just the right notes.

ginger

curry

Here it is: the answer your grilling prayers. Just pick your main ingredient, and then let Lemonology lead the way. It all comes down to six essential elements that transform simplicity into bliss. A grill girl's taste buds lust after garlic and olive oil, beg for herbal aromas, and crave the crunch of salt and cracked pepper. Lemon, O'Mighty Lemon, has the power and bite to fuse them all together. Know this is The One. Use freely, spontaneously, frequently.

Lemonology:
A theory of vital ingredients

Zest of 1 lemon

2 tablespoons fresh lemon juice

1/3 cup olive oil

1/4 teaspoon kosher salt

1/2 teaspoon coarsely ground pepper

2 cloves garlic, minced

2 tablespoons chopped fresh rosemary

In a 1-cup glass measure, combine the lemon zest, lemon juice, olive oil, salt, and pepper. Stir until the salt is dissolved. Add the garlic and rosemary. Taste and adjust the flavors: If you're a gutsy gal, pump up the garlic. This marinade is best made fresh. As a rule, foods should only marinate at room temperature up to 1 hour; beyond this, refrigerate.

MARINATING TIMES: Shrimp and scallops, 30 minutes; fish steaks or fillets, 30 to 60 minutes; chicken breasts and thighs, 1 to 2 hours; beef or lamb kebabs, 1 to 2 hours; pork chops and tenderloin, 1 to 2 hours; vegetables, 30 to 60 minutes. Remove from marinade and grill as desired.

● Makes about 1/2 cup

cook and tell
Change the mood and the mode by replacing rosemary with basil. Or try a mixture of fresh herbs, such as equal portions of basil, oregano, and thyme, plus something unexpected, perhaps lavender or lemon mint.

Think of this as a mud bath for your favorite grill foods: thick, heady, and tingly at first, but, in the end, totally fresh and vibrant.

Mod bods

mustard marinade

¹/₂ cup **Dijon mustard**

3 tablespoons olive oil

1 tablespoon dried tarragon leaves, crushed

¹/₂ teaspoon freshly ground pepper

It doesn't get simpler than this: In a small bowl, whisk together all the ingredients. Use immediately, or cover and refrigerate up to 1 month. As a rule, foods should only marinate at room temperature up to 1 hour. Beyond this, refrigerate.

MARINATING TIMES: Whole chicken, 1 hour; chicken parts, 15 to 60 minutes; lamb chops or butterflied leg of lamb, 30 to 60 minutes. Grill the coated meats as desired.

● Makes about ²/₃ cup

cook and tell
You don't wear the same lipstick every day, so why get stuck on one mustard? A whole world of colors and taste sensations is worth exploring, from spicy, chocolate-brown *mole* mustard to sharp, pale green tarragon mustard. Either eliminate the tarragon or try another complementary herb for a personalized flavor stamp.

Good fortune comes to those who combine nine classic Asian accents and watch them magically create a thousand layers of sweet, smoky, and pungent flavors.

Hidden pleasures

hoisin-ginger glaze

1 cup hoisin sauce

1/2 cup plum sauce

1/2 cup low-sodium soy sauce

1/4 cup pale, dry sherry

1/4 cup Asian sesame oil

2 tablespoons minced fresh ginger

1 1/2 tablespoons minced garlic

1 teaspoon freshly ground pepper

1/4 cup honey

In a medium bowl combine all the ingredients. Stir thoroughly to blend. Use immediately, or cover and refrigerate up to 1 month. (Your fortune cookie should read: Leftover glaze brings easy meal next time.) As a rule, foods should only marinate at room temperature up to 1 hour; beyond this, refrigerate.

MARINATING TIMES: Baby back ribs, 6 to 8 hours or overnight; whole chicken, 6 to 8 hours; chicken parts including wings, 6 to 8 hours; pork tenderloin, 2 to 4 hours. Grill the coated meats as desired.

● Makes about 3 cups

cook and tell
Do a power mince of lots of fresh ginger. Pack the extra in a jar, cover with sherry, and refrigerate up to 2 months. Working now pays off later, bringing good luck to the harried cook.

Our spin on charmoula, *a traditional Moroccan mari-nade, thickens the waters to create an oily paste that's at once feisty and tart, garlicky and deliriously cilantro-ed, with a delayed power surge of cumin.*

Forbidden nights
Moroccan pesto

$^1/_4$ **cup coarsely chopped fresh parsley**

$^3/_4$ **cup coarsely chopped fresh cilantro**

5 large cloves garlic

1$^1/_2$ teaspoons each: kosher salt, paprika, and ground cumin

$^1/_2$ **teaspoon dried thyme**

$^1/_4$ **teaspoon cayenne pepper**

$^1/_3$ **cup fresh lemon juice**

$^1/_3$ **cup olive oil**

In a food processor fitted with the metal blade, combine the parsley, cilantro, and garlic; process to a coarse paste. Add the salt, paprika, cumin, thyme, and cayenne; process until combined. Add the lemon juice and olive oil. Process until the mixture forms a paste. Tinker with the heat level if you wish, but don't stray into palate-obliterating territory. Though best when used immediately, the pesto will hold 2 or 3 days if covered and refrigerated. As a rule, foods should only marinate at room temperature up to 1 hour; beyond this, refrigerate.

MARINATING TIMES: Whole chicken, 3 to 4 hours; chicken parts, 2 to 4 hours; lamb chops or butterflied leg of lamb, 2 to 4 hours; fish fillets or shrimp, 2 to 3 hours; vegetables, 30 to 60 minutes. Grill the coated foods as desired.

● Makes about 1$^1/_4$ cups

cook and tell

Cilantro is a pungent herb that tastes like manna to some, soap to others. It's the defining note here, so love it or leave it, but don't leave it out.

If you can stand the heat, get into your kitchen and whip up our lip-buzzing spice blend, guaranteed to jump-start any backyard grill fest. Bring it on, sister.

Hot girls
spice rub

1/4 cup kosher salt

2 tablespoons coarsely ground pepper

1 tablespoon ground coriander

3 tablespoons ground cumin

2 tablespoons each: paprika, dried thyme, and chili powder

1/4 cup packed dark brown sugar

2 teaspoons ground cinnamon

Combine all the ingredients in a bowl. Stir well to blend. Store in an airtight jar away from heat or light. The rub will keep for up to 6 months, which is longer than many relationships. As a rule, foods should only marinate at room temperature up to 1 hour; beyond this, refrigerate.

MARINATING TIMES: Shrimp and scallops, 15 minutes; chicken breasts and thighs, 30 to 60 minutes; beef or lamb kebabs, 1 hour; pork chops and tenderloin, 45 to 60 minutes. Grill the rubbed foods as desired.

● Makes 1¹/4 cups

cook and tell
Quadruple the recipe for a summer's worth of soul-satisfying grilling. How sweet it is.

Whether flaming out on a relationship or sparking a new romance, you need a rush of something, so it might as well be the mysterious and intriguing ingredients of the East. This combo is meant to sear and seduce the palate.

Burning desire:
An Indonesian blend

1 or 2 serrano chiles, including seeds, minced

1 stalk of fresh lemongrass, tender inner bulb only, minced

3 cloves garlic, minced

3 tablespoons minced fresh ginger

1/4 cup shredded unsweetened coconut

Zest of 2 limes

1/3 cup fresh lime juice

3 tablespoons *nam pla* (fish sauce)

1/3 cup Asian sesame oil

In a medium bowl, combine all the ingredients and stir thoroughly to blend. Use immediately, or cover and refrigerate up to 2 weeks. As a rule, foods should only marinate at room temperature up to 1 hour; beyond this, refrigerate.

MARINATING TIMES: Shrimp, 2 to 4 hours; whole chicken, 6 to 8 hours; chicken parts including wings, 4 to 6 hours; chicken kebabs, 2 hours; fish fillets or kebabs, 1 to 3 hours. Grill the coated foods as desired.

cook and tell
Recycle savvy: Stick the long stem of the lemongrass with a few tropical flowers for an instant centerpiece.

● Makes 1 1/2 cups

Jerk paste is to Jamaican wood pits what barbecue sauce is to American grills, or for that matter, what hot fudge sauce is to a girl's psyche: truth and soul, a way of life, a signature of its creator. Jerk, of course, has other connotations, and this smoldering paste does double-duty when you're feeling a slow burn and want to wallow in it.

Jerk paste

2 to 4 Scotch bonnet or habanero chiles, including seeds, quartered

1 small yellow onion, quartered

3 green onions (white and green parts), cut into 1-inch lengths

4 quarter-size slices fresh ginger

3 cloves garlic

1/2 cup packed coarsely chopped fresh cilantro

2 tablespoons kosher salt

1 tablespoon each: ground allspice, dried thyme, and coarsely ground pepper

1/4 cup packed dark brown sugar

1/4 cup fresh lime juice

1/4 cup soy sauce

2 tablespoons vegetable oil

In a food processor fitted with the metal blade, combine the chiles, yellow onion, green onions, ginger, garlic, and cilantro; process to a coarse paste. Add the salt, allspice, thyme, pepper, and brown sugar; process until combined. Then add the lime juice, soy sauce, and oil. Process until the mixture forms a paste. Use immediately, or transfer to a jar with a tight-fitting lid and refrigerate up to 1 month. As a rule, foods should only marinate at room temperature up to 1 hour—the maximum amount of time you should cry over any jerk; beyond this, refrigerate.

MARINATING TIMES: Whole chicken, 3 to 4 hours; chicken parts, 2 to 4 hours; pork chops or pork tenderloin, 2 to 4 hours; fish fillets or shrimp, 1 hour. Grill the coated foods as desired.

● Makes 2 cups

cook and tell

The oils from hot peppers permeate the skin of your hands. Absentmindedly touching your nose or eyes after handling the peppers is going to be more painful than the first lonely night. Get yourself some disposable surgical gloves—just be sure to remove them before guests arrive so they don't get the wrong impression.

Perfume your kitchen with sweet and pungent smells,
the culinary equivalent of burning temple incense.
What better way to purge the scent of his aftershave?

Sisters of the revenge
Indian spice rub

1 tablespoon cumin seeds

1 tablespoon coriander seeds

1 tablespoon fennel seeds

1 tablespoon kosher salt

2 tablespoons curry powder

1/4 to 1/2 teaspoon cayenne pepper

4 large cloves garlic

1/4 cup fresh lemon juice

2 tablespoons vegetable oil

In a small, heavy skillet, preferably cast iron, toast the cumin, coriander, and fennel seeds over high heat, stirring, until fragrant and lightly browned, about 2 minutes. Cool on a plate. Deeply inhale the aromas, and imagine him being prodded across burning coals at a fraudulent yogi retreat in Bombay.

Place the seeds in a blender and whirl until ground to a powder. Add the salt, curry powder, cayenne, and garlic. Blend to a paste. Add the lemon juice and oil, and blend to combine. As a rule, foods should only marinate at room temperature up to 1 hour; beyond this, refrigerate.

MARINATING TIMES: Chicken parts and kebabs, 2 to 4 hours; fish fillets or shrimp, 1 hour. Grill the coated foods as desired.

● Makes 1/2 cup

cook and tell
Dry-roasting whole spices in a skillet and then grinding them is the ancient way of maximizing the potential of flavor and scent. The wise make the effort.

The
light stuff

Grilling the low-fat way

Diet, schmiet. Don't sweat the inches and pounds, and forget mourning last year's dress size. Be in the moment. Eat here now. We'd be the last ones to tell anyone to forgo their calorie catastrophes. Still, girls like to be smart, have options, and know where to make their trade-offs. Chocolate milkshake and fries for lunch; a waist-watching salad with grilled prawns for dinner. Pancakes with an entire sky of whipped cream on Saturday morning, and by nightfall, a rescue of spicy gazpacho. You get the picture here: It's a balancing act. No gain, no pain.

Calorie-busting gazpacho with seared scallops

Waistland salad

Svelte salmon with fig balsamic sauce

Forget Caesar: A bang-up Cleopatra salad

Ahi tuna: Raw, raw, sizzlin' boom bah

Grilled halibut with mambo queens mango salsa

Ragin' hormones-free chicken

When penne met portobella

In this spin on the Spanish classic, the cucumbers are out and chunklets of tomatoes are in, dancing around a purée of big, smoky flavors, which broadcasts basil's irresistible perfume, a powerful whiff of garlic, and the sensuality of plump, delicately seared scallops. Serve in big martini glasses, feel swank, and know your bod is thanking you.

Calorie-busting
gazpacho

GAZPACHO
2 large cloves garlic

1^1/$_2$ teaspoons sugar

^{1}/$_4$ teaspoon cayenne pepper

1 slice day-old bread, torn into small pieces

^{1}/$_2$ bunch watercress, or 2 outer romaine leaves

^{1}/$_4$ cup rice wine or white wine vinegar

2 tablespoons olive oil

6 large fresh basil leaves

1 can (14^1/$_2$ ounces) beef or vegetable broth

6 medium tomatoes, cored, seeded, and cut into ^{1}/$_4$-inch dice

2 cups **V8** juice

Kosher salt and freshly ground pepper

12 fresh sea scallops, cleaned and blotted dry

2 tablespoons olive oil

Salt and freshly ground pepper

3 (10-inch-long) bamboo skewers, soaked in water for 30 minutes, then drained

Vegetable oil for brushing

2 tablespoons minced fresh chives

with seared scallops

To make the gazpacho: In a food processor or blender, purée the garlic, sugar, cayenne, and bread. As you pulse and whirl, stand up straight and tall and squeeze buns tight. (This calorie-sparing recipe can't do all the work.) Trim away any tough watercress stems, or remove the thick spines of the romaine leaves. Add the watercress or romaine to the work bowl. Add the vinegar, oil, basil, and beef or vegetable broth. Process until puréed (squeeze, 2, 3, 4). Transfer to a large bowl and stir in the tomatoes and V8 juice. Add salt and pepper to taste. Cover and chill until ready to serve.

To cook the scallops: Prepare a medium-hot fire in a charcoal grill or preheat a gas or electric grill on medium-high. In a bowl, toss the scallops with the olive oil and a little salt and pepper. Set aside for 15 minutes, then thread 4 scallops onto each skewer. Brush the grill grate with vegetable oil. Grill the scallops directly over medium-high heat until nicely browned outside and just opaque inside, about 2 minutes per side. Remove and slide them off the skewers.

Stir the soup and ladle into martini glasses. Feel hip, and while you're at it, move yours: Sway vigorously four times. Then garnish each glass with 2 grilled scallops and some minced chives.

cook and tell

Ingredients can come and go, but the right bread is a bottom-line gazpacho ingredient. Don't even consider one of those nine-grain sprouted wheat numbers. Crusty country bread is the ticket.

● Serves 6

A one-dish wonder: all manner of crunchy things mingled with spicy shrimp and a calorie-forgiving dressing that will leave your mouth feeling indulged and your waistline intact.

Waistland salad

1 pound large shrimp, shelled and deveined

3 tablespoons Hot Girls Spice Rub (page 28)

Vegetable oil for brushing

1/2 cup slivered almonds

8 cups torn romaine lettuce leaves

1 large Anaheim chile, halved lengthwise, seeded, and cut crosswise into thin slices

8 ounces jicama, peeled and cut into matchsticks

1/2 cup chopped fresh cilantro

1 large navel orange, peeled and cut into thin wedges

DRESSING
1/4 cup each: reduced-fat sour cream and light mayonnaise

2 tablespoons fresh orange juice

1/2 teaspoon each: kosher salt and sugar

Freshly ground pepper

Prepare a hot fire in a charcoal grill or preheat a gas or electric grill on high. In a medium bowl, toss the shrimp with the spice rub and set aside for 15 minutes. (Confession: Our fabuloso rub will get under your nails. Use a nailbrush and get over it—these shrimp are worth it.) Brush the grill grate with vegetable oil. Grill the shrimp directly over high heat until just opaque, about 2 minutes per side. Remove and set aside.

Meanwhile, preheat the oven to 350°F. Spread the almonds on a rimmed baking sheet and bake until lightly browned, about 8 to 10 minutes. Set aside to cool. If you're fat obsessed—you know who you are—omit the nuts. (But don't go behind our backs and sneak a Snickers later.)

In a large salad bowl, toss together the lettuce, chile, jicama, cilantro, and orange wedges.

To make the dressing: In a small bowl, combine the sour cream, mayonnaise, orange juice, salt, sugar, and pepper to taste.

cook and tell
Use a little wave-o-magic to save time: Toast the nuts in the microwave on high until lightly browned, about 3 minutes.

Add the toasted almonds and grilled shrimp to the salad bowl. Add the dressing and toss with the salad. Serve immediately.

● Serves 4 to 6 as a main-course salad

When you're working on your silhouette, nothing could be finer than a recipe stripped down to its elegant basics: a sleek fillet grilled to perfection with nothing more than salt, pepper, and a thick, black-purple vinegar that tastes of earth and autumn.

Svelte salmon with fig balsamic sauce

4 salmon fillets, 1/2 inch thick (about 6 ounces each)

3 tablespoons olive oil

Kosher salt and freshly ground pepper

Vegetable oil for brushing

1/2 cup balsamic vinegar with figs

Prepare a medium-hot fire in a charcoal grill or preheat a gas or electric grill on medium-high.

Rub the salmon fillets with the oil and sprinkle with salt and pepper to taste. When the grill is hot, brush the grill grate with vegetable oil.

Place the salmon, skin-side up, directly over the medium-hot fire. Cover the grill and cook the salmon on one side, about 5 minutes. Turn and cover again. Cook about 5 minutes more, or until opaque all the way through, or an instant-read thermometer registers 130°F. Serve immediately with a couple of tablespoons of fig balsamic spooned to one side of each fillet. (What could be more beautiful than a "sauce" straight from the bottle? Life doesn't get better than this. All you need is a nice Beaujolais and some pals to share it with.)

cook and tell
Look for balsamic vinegar with figs in specialty food stores. It's also terrific with grilled pork or in a salad dressing, mixed with extra-virgin olive oil.

● Serves 4

The classic the way it was meant to be, garlic fragrant, anchovy sly, and elegantly adorned with a pyramid of sliced lemon-grilled chicken.

Forget Caesar: A bang-up

MARINADE

$^1/_3$ cup olive oil

$1^1/_2$ tablespoons fresh
lemon juice

$^1/_2$ teaspoon kosher salt

Freshly ground pepper

1 large clove garlic,
minced

6 boneless, skinless
chicken breasts

DRESSING

1 tablespoon minced garlic

2 oil-packed anchovy fillets, patted dry
and minced, or 1 tablespoon anchovy
paste

$^3/_4$ teaspoon kosher salt

2 tablespoons fresh lemon juice

1 very fresh large egg

$^1/_2$ cup extra-virgin olive oil

$^1/_4$ cup freshly grated Parmigiano-
Reggiano cheese, plus extra for
garnish

3 heads romaine lettuce, well chilled

Vegetable oil for brushing

$1^1/_2$ cups homemade or store-bought
large croutons

Freshly ground pepper

Cleopatra salad

To make the marinade: In a small bowl, whisk together all the marinade ingredients. Place the chicken in a baking dish. Add the marinade. Set aside for 30 minutes at room temperature.

To make the dressing: In a small bowl, whisk together the garlic, anchovies, salt, and lemon juice. Add the egg, whisking the dressing until thick, about 1 minute. Slowly drizzle in the oil, whisking vigorously to thicken. Whisk in the cheese. Taste and adjust the flavor. Set aside.

Separate the romaine leaves, discarding the coarse outer leaves and saving the inner leaves and hearts. Keep the leaves whole.

cook and tell

If you prefer to avoid raw eggs, substitute 1 additional tablespoon of olive oil in place of the egg.

Prepare a hot fire in a charcoal grill or preheat a gas or electric grill on high. Brush the grill grate with vegetable oil. Place the chicken breasts directly over the hot fire. Cover the grill and cook the chicken on one side, about 4 minutes. Turn and cover again. Cook about 4 more minutes, or until the juices run clear when pierced with a knife, or an instant-read thermometer registers 165°F. Set aside.

To assemble: Pour half of the dressing in the bottom of an oversized mixing bowl. Add the croutons and toss in the dressing until thoroughly coated. Add the lettuce leaves and hearts, and the remaining dressing. Toss just until coated. Divide among 6 entrée plates. Thinly slice the chicken breasts and arrange pyramid-style over the top. Garnish with additional cheese and freshly ground pepper. Serve immediately. This is finger food—meant to be eaten royally, one leaf at a time.

● Serves 6

We rally around rare tuna steaks—sweet, mildly oceanic, and with a flash of grill flavor. A coat of crushed peppercorns and a final flourish of black olive tapenade add just the right of amount of pep, without adding a calorie overload.

Ahi tuna: Raw, raw, sizzlin' boom bah

2 tablespoons extra-virgin olive oil

1/3 cup store-bought black olive tapenade

2 tablespoons kosher salt

1/3 cup coarsely crushed black peppercorns

4 ahi tuna steaks, 1 1/4 inches thick (about 5 ounces each)

Vegetable oil for brushing

Thoroughly combine the olive oil and tapenade. Set aside.

Prepare a hot fire in a charcoal grill or preheat a gas or electric grill on high. Mix the salt and crushed peppercorns together and spread out on a dinner plate. Press each tuna steak into the mixture until heavily coated on both sides. (Do this while chanting to the diet gods: 2-4-6-8 who do we appreciate? Tu-*na*. tu-*na*. tu-*na*.) Set aside on a plate.

When ready to grill, brush the grill grate with vegetable oil. Place the steaks directly over the hot fire. Cover the grill and cook the steaks on one side for 2 minutes. Turn and cover again. Cook about 2 minutes, or until still red-rare in the center, or an instant-read thermometer registers 120°F when inserted into the steak's center.

cook and tell
Freshly ground pepper is the winning flavor in just about every savory recipe. Time to get rid of the bottled stuff and buy a pepper mill. Grinding pepper works the biceps. You grind, girl.

Pour a spoonful of olive sauce on each steak. Step to your left, step to your right, serve immediately, you're lookin' alright.

● Serves 4

Fish with all the right moves: moist within,
magnificently charred without, and boasting a
hip-swaying, fruity-hot salsa to spark the flames.

Grilled halibut with
mambo queens
mango salsa

MANGO SALSA
1 tablespoon olive oil

1/2 teaspoon each: ground cumin and ground coriander

2 large firm, ripe mangoes, peeled and diced

1/4 cup finely diced red onion

1 jalapeño chile, seeded and minced

1/4 cup chopped fresh cilantro

1/4 teaspoon kosher salt

1 tablespoon fresh lime juice

4 halibut steaks, 1 inch thick (about 8 ounces each)

2 tablespoons olive oil

Kosher salt and freshly ground pepper

Vegetable oil for brushing

You always did want salsa lessons, so here goes: Pop in a blistering CD of salsa king Tito Puente. Listen carefully to the beat. Count in a series of eight. Down a margarita. Exaggerate the motion of your hips, and make like Millie Donay, the legendary dancer who put the sex in salsa in the '50s. (You may need to work up to this.) Meanwhile, between moves, combine the oil, cumin, and coriander in a small bowl. Set aside. Next step: In a medium bowl, combine the mangoes, onion, jalapeño, cilantro, salt, and lime juice. Add the reserved oil and spice mixture, and stir well to combine. Set aside for 1 hour before serving.

Prepare a medium-hot fire in a charcoal grill or preheat a gas or electric grill on medium-high. Rub the fish with the olive oil and season with salt and pepper to taste. Set aside on a plate.

When ready to grill, brush the grill grate with vegetable oil. Place the steaks directly over the medium-hot fire. Cover the grill and cook the steaks on one side for 5 minutes. Turn and cover again. Cook 5 or 6 minutes, or until opaque throughout, or an instant-read thermometer registers 125°F when inserted into the steak's center.

Spoon a couple of tablespoons of salsa over each steak. Serve immediately.

● Serves 4

cook and tell
Start dancin' early. The salsa gets better with time and can be made 1 day in advance.

Yes, they do cost more. But free-range chickens are tastier, meatier, and maybe less moody than their hormones-charged, cooped-up cousins. Your mood will certainly improve when you taste this flavor-intensive, calorie-sparing bird, with assertive North African spices pulsating through its bronzed skin.

Ragin'

hormones-free chicken

1 free-range chicken (4 to 4¹/2 pounds), cut into 8 pieces

Place the chicken pieces in a 1-gallon resealable plastic bag or in a shallow baking pan.

1¹/4 cups Forbidden Nights Moroccan Pesto (page 27)

Vegetable oil for brushing

Coat the chicken with the Moroccan Pesto. Seal the bag or cover the pan and refrigerate 2 to 4 hours. Turn the bag or rotate the chicken pieces occasionally to coat all sides. Remove from the refrigerator 30 minutes before grilling.

Prepare a medium-hot fire in a charcoal grill or preheat a gas or electric grill on medium-high. Brush the grill grate with vegetable oil.

Place the coated chicken directly over the medium-hot fire. Cover the grill and cook the chicken on one side, about 12 minutes. Turn and cover again. Cook about 12 minutes more, or until the juices run clear when pierced with a knife, or an instant-read thermometer registers 165°F when inserted into the thickest part of the breast and thigh. Serve immediately or keep warm.

cook and tell

Resealable plastic bags make marinating a snap. The ingredients can be massaged and completely coated in the bag—and there's no pan to clean.

● Serves 4 to 6

*It was the beginning of a great pasta affair, especially
when grilled sweet onions got into the middle. They all
melded happily in a bowl when the vinegar got wild
with the mushrooms and the cheese partied on top.*

When penne met portobella

**4 large portobella
mushrooms**

**1 large Walla Walla
or Vidalia sweet
onion, thickly
sliced into rounds**

**1/2 cup plus 2 table-
spoons olive oil**

**2 tablespoons
balsamic vinegar**

**1 pound penne
pasta**

Zest of 1 lemon

**1 tablespoon minced
fresh thyme**

**1/2 cup minced fresh
parsley**

**Kosher salt and
freshly ground
pepper**

**1/3 cup freshly
grated
Parmigiano-
Reggiano cheese**

Prepare a hot fire in a charcoal grill or preheat a gas or electric grill on high. Stem the mushrooms and wipe the caps
clean with a damp paper towel. Use a spoon to scoop away
the dark brown gills from the undersides of the portobellas—
otherwise, they will blacken and look nasty when grilled
(the "ick" factor). Brush both sides of the onion slices and
mushroom caps with the 1/2 cup olive oil.

Grill the vegetables directly over the hot fire, turning once,
until nicely browned, 5 to 7 minutes per side. Halve the
mushrooms, and slice cross-
wise into thin strips. Place in
a mixing bowl and toss with
the vinegar. Coarsely chop
the grilled onions. Set aside.

Cook the pasta according to
package directions. Be sure
to taste for that perfecto, al
dente stage, when the pasta
is tender but still has some
bite. Drain and place in a
serving bowl. Toss with the 2 tablespoons olive oil.
Add the grilled vegetables, plus any remaining liquid in the
mixing bowl. Add the lemon zest, thyme, parsley, and salt
and pepper to taste. Sprinkle the cheese over the top. Serve
immediately.

cook and tell
Grilled portobellas are
the steaks of the vege-
tarian world. Nothing
makes their flavor rock
better than a big splash
of balsamic vinegar,
brushed on right after
the mushrooms come
off the grill.

● Serves 4 or 5

43

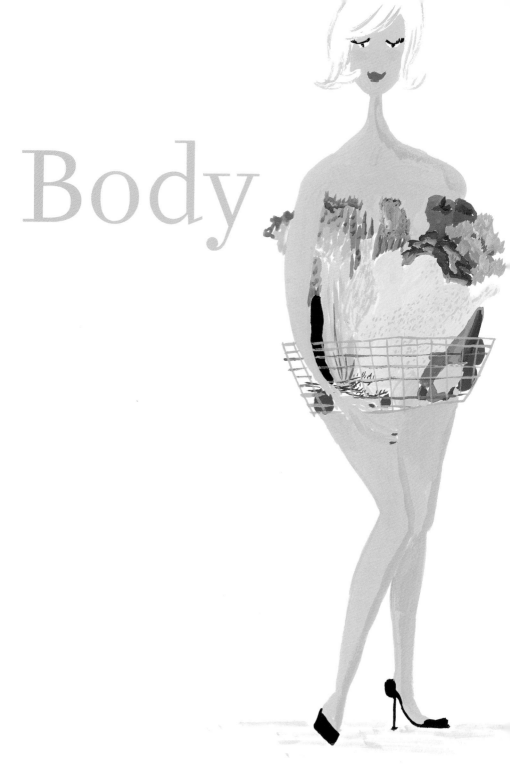

Body

work

Showing off the best parts

We're not exactly talking about fitness. The point here is a hot excursion across the sexier contours of food. These dishes come with their own allure, their own points of desire—from a killer leg of lamb to the provocative curves of baby back ribs to the voluptuous lines of a classic chicken breast. You don't have to be Catherine Zeta-Jones to put together our list of carnal ingredients for a night too steamy to forget.

Getting naked
Firm thighs
Great legs
What a back

Pale, soft, and smooth. Gently massaged with sharp mustard-and-herbal oil. What could be more beautifully naked in its simplicity?

Getting naked

4 to 6 boneless, skinless chicken breast halves

$^1/_2$ to $^2/_3$ cup Mod Bods Mustard Marinade (page 25)

Vegetable oil for brushing

Prepare a hot fire in a charcoal grill or preheat a gas or electric grill on high. Pound the chicken breasts lightly between two pieces of plastic wrap. (Whoa, girlfriend. Be gentler than the techs clamping down on the old mammogram machine.) Place them in a shallow baking dish and slather the marinade evenly over both sides. Marinate at least 15 minutes or up to 1 hour at room temperature.

Brush the grill grate with vegetable oil. Remove the chicken from the marinade and place directly over the hot fire. Cover the grill and cook on one side about 4 minutes. The breasts will plump up just like yours in a push-up bra. Turn and cover again. Cook about 4 minutes more, or until the juices run clear when pierced with a knife, or an instant-read thermometer registers 165°F. Serve immediately.

● Serves 4 to 6

cook and tell

Forget eye-popping garnishes. It's enough to serve the breasts slightly overlapped on a platter for that can't-keep-your-eyes-off-cleavage look.

Show off these babies in a sauce that brings to mind slinky short-shorts, bustling outdoor markets, and the festive flavors of Oaxaca. This is the home of mole, a thick and wondrous paste of Mexican spices electrified by dark chocolate and the aroma of simmering cilantro. When the chicken and mole come together with a serving of mashed potatoes (page 55), you know you have tasted the divine.

Firm thighs

8 chicken thighs

¹/3 cup Hot Girls Spice Rub (page 28)

MOLE SAUCE
¹/4 cup store-bought *mole*, such as Doña Maria

1 cup canned low-sodium chicken broth

¹/2 ounce bittersweet chocolate, chopped

1 pinch each: kosher salt and sugar

¹/4 teaspoon ground cinnamon

Vegetable oil for brushing

Rub the chicken all over with the Hot Girls Spice Rub. Go deep and in a circular motion, as if you were applying a good exfoliating body scrub. Marinate 45 minutes at room temperature. Meanwhile, prepare a medium fire in a charcoal grill or preheat a gas or electric grill on medium. You will want to dive into a side of hot, buttery spuds, so . . . take 20 minutes and work your thighs.

In a small saucepan, combine the Mole Sauce ingredients. Cook over low heat, stirring frequently, until the chocolate melts and the sauce is well blended. Simmer 10 minutes, then cover and keep warm.

cook and tell
Mole is available at Latin American markets, specialty food stores, and some supermarkets. Use our doctored sauce on anything from enchiladas to sliced turkey.

Brush the grill grate with vegetable oil. Place the chicken thighs, skin-side down, directly over the medium fire. Cover the grill and cook the chicken on one side, about 10 minutes. Move the chicken away from the direct heat if you are experiencing flare-ups. Turn and cover again. Cook about 8 to 10 minutes, or until the juices run clear when pierced with a knife, or an instant-read thermometer registers 165°F.

Spoon enough Mole Sauce on each plate to lightly cover the surface. Mound with some mashed potatoes if you like, and place two thighs on top. Serve immediately.

● Serves 4

There's more than one way to get killer gams. Consider this lamb the Tina Turner of the grill universe: dynamic and shapely. Garlic sings the loud notes, and the meat is as rare as an indestructible silky sheer stocking.

Great legs

1 boned and butter-flied leg of lamb, 4 to 5 pounds

1/2 cup olive oil

6 large cloves garlic, minced

1 teaspoon kosher salt

2 teaspoons freshly ground pepper

1/4 cup dried oregano

1/4 cup dried rosemary, crumbled

Vegetable oil for brushing

Lay the butterflied lamb leg flat on a cutting board, skin-side up. Trim away any skin and fat. (Ah, were it that easy.) Place in a shallow pan large enough for the lamb to lie flat. A few leg lifts will help get it in place (10 for you won't hurt, either).

Combine the olive oil, garlic, salt, and pepper. Coat all sides of the lamb with the mixture. Marinate at room temperature for 1 hour.

Prepare a medium-hot fire in a charcoal grill or preheat a gas or electric grill on medium-high.

Remove the lamb from the marinade. Coat one side with oregano, the other with rosemary. Brush the grill grate with vegetable oil. Grill the lamb directly over the medium-hot fire, covered, for 15 minutes on one side. Turn and grill about 15 minutes longer, or until medium-rare, or when an instant-read thermometer inserted in the meat's thickest part registers 120° to 130°F. Let rest 10 minutes. Carve across the grain into thin slices.

● Serves 10 to 12

cook and tell

Let your butcher be the plastic surgeon: Order the meat butterflied, skinned, and trimmed.

The curvature is perfect: no flab at the spine, and so nice for nibbling, especially the crunchy, charred edges around threads of tender meat. The silky-sweet hoisin glaze pumped up with ginger and garlic is meant for licking.

What a back

3 racks pork baby back ribs (about 1¹/2 pounds each)

3 cups Hidden Pleasures Hoisin-Ginger Glaze (page 26)

3 cups hickory or apple wood chips

Disposable foil pan

Vegetable oil for brushing

Place the ribs flat in a nonreactive roasting pan, or "roll" the racks and fit them into a 1¹/2-gallon resealable plastic bag. Set aside ¹/2 cup of the glaze. Pour the remaining glaze over the ribs, rubbing it onto both sides like a good back massage. (Get one yourself while the ribs are relaxing in the glaze. Beg, plead, or threaten to withhold ribs.) Cover the pan with plastic wrap or tightly seal the bag. Refrigerate 6 to 8 hours to blend the flavors.

Soak the wood chips in cold water to cover for 1 hour. Set up the grill for indirect cooking (see page 20). Prepare a medium fire in a charcoal grill or preheat one side of a gas or electric grill on medium. Drain the chips and sprinkle half of them over the coals, or place half in the grill's smoker box. Place a disposable foil pan under the grate to catch drippings.

cook and tell
Leave the smoked-all-day spare ribs to the dudes. Pork baby backs are sweet and tender and good to go by the time you've exchanged war stories from the relationship front.

Brush the grill grate with vegetable oil. Arrange the ribs, meaty-side down, on the side of the grill without hot coals. Cover the grill and smoke-cook the ribs 45 minutes. Turn the ribs and add the remaining wood chips. Cover and grill another 45 minutes. Brush the ribs with half of the reserved glaze. Using long-handled tongs, slide the ribs onto the grate directly over the hot coals. Grill, uncovered, 5 minutes. Turn the ribs over, baste again, and grill another 5 minutes. Cut between the bones, slicing the racks into individual ribs. Serve immediately.

● Serves 4 to 6

5

Dishes of
desire

Le hot date

Remember this as you're sweating off your makeup by the oven door, wondering why you didn't order take-out. This is the ultimate grill dinner, and it's only replayed if he turns out to be really worth it. We cover the bases here (no, not the ones he wants to tag): the mood-setting martini, the essential hunk of beef, the dessert to make Freud proud— Mom's apple pie, and then some. Believe it, girl, he'll be back on his hands and knees begging for more. Let's hope you still want him.

Boy toy martini

Animal magnetism: The steak and the sizzle

Better than his mom's mashed potatoes

Think big and long: grilled asparagus

Hey, I bake biscuits, too!

Guy pie

Don't mess with his mind here. Save that for later. Stick to the classic, real-deal formula, guaranteed to release his inner Martini Man: gin of the highest order, vermouth that speaks only in whispers, and everything numbingly cold. Then, stir like Madonna vogues: with style, purpose, and knowing eyes. (Intelligence report: Do not even mention the "shake" word.)

Boy toy martini

4 pitted green olives

2¹/₂ cups cracked ice

7 ounces top-quality gin, such as Bombay Sapphire or Tanqueray

1 ounce dry vermouth, preferably Noilly Prat

Rinse two 6-ounce martini glasses with cold water and place them in the freezer until ready to serve.

Spear the olives, two to a cocktail pick or plastic sword. Set aside.

Place the ice in a tall mixing glass or one of those martini pitchers with a molded lip designed to keep the ice from splaying all over the place, not to mention your dress. Add the gin and vermouth. With a long-handled bar spoon, stir very gently to chill (martini fanatics believe you can "bruise" the ice if your movements

are too brisk—let's hope your date is not one of them). Or just swirl the ingredients in the glass. Either way, work quickly so the ice doesn't melt and—heaven forbid—dilute the gin. When frost sticks to your fingers and the liquid has a slightly glassy shimmer, the martini is ready.

Remove the glasses from the freezer. Strain the gin and vermouth evenly between the 2 glasses. Garnish each with an olive spear and serve.

● Serves 2

stir and tell

It's all about confidence, quick hands, and ritual observance. Play it cool: Stash the mixing glass—even the shot glass— in the deep freeze, and chill the vermouth in the fridge. Know the game, and he'll be shaken and stirred.

Steak the way it was meant to be: stripped down to its primal, lusty essence. In short, a hunk. No sauce, no "trendoid" garnishes. Just juicy, rare, and tender, with a seared-in salt crust that layers the textural sensations.

Animal magnetism:
The steak and the sizzle

2 tablespoons kosher or sea salt

¹/4 cup coarsely crushed black peppercorns

2 New York strip steaks, 1¹/2 inches thick (about 12 ounces each), preferably Angus or USDA Prime aged beef

Vegetable oil for brushing

Remember: It's all about technique and good-lookin' marbled meat. Prepare a hot fire in a charcoal grill or preheat a gas or electric grill on high. Combine the salt and crushed peppercorns and coat the top and bottom of each steak, massaging ever so lightly. Set aside on a plate. No scoring—the beef, that is—even if he insists.

Brush the grill grate with vegetable oil. Place the steaks directly over the hot fire. Two choices here: rare or medium-rare. Period. If he's the well-done type, make the night short and quick-kiss him goodbye—he's got no taste. Cover the grill and cook the steaks on one side, 5 minutes for rare to 7 minutes for medium-rare. Turn, cover again, and cook 5 minutes more. Whip out your instant-read thermometer and check the temp—120°F for rare (warm and red in the center) or 130° to 135°F for medium-rare (pink in the center). Let the steaks rest for 3 minutes before serving.

● Serves 2

cook and tell
An instant-read thermometer is an absolute must for perfectly cooked steaks. It costs the same as a good lipstick. No excuses. Just get one.

Creamy, dreamy, back-to-the-womb spuds, rich with—
no other way to say it—butter.

Better than his
mom's mashed potatoes

2 large russet potatoes (about 1 pound total)

1 teaspoon kosher salt, plus extra for seasoning

1/2 cup milk

5 tablespoons unsalted butter

Freshly ground pepper

2 to 3 drops truffle oil

Peel the potatoes (watch those pampered nails—hey, you paid for them!!). Rinse under cold water and cut each into quarters. Place in a medium saucepan and cover with cold water. Partially cover the pot and bring the water to a boil. Uncover, add the 1 teaspoon salt, and reduce the heat so the water boils gently. Cook until the potatoes are tender when pierced with a fork, about 10 to 12 minutes.

Meanwhile, in a small saucepan, heat the milk until hot but not boiling. In another small saucepan, melt the butter. We've given an amount here, but there's no such thing as too much butter.

Drain the potatoes. Want to avoid watery potatoes? Return them to the warm pan and place over low heat for 1 minute to evaporate any excess water. Use a potato masher to break up the potatoes (call it your day's upper-body workout). Or, for that ultra-smooth-guy texture, use a ricer. Stir the butter into the potatoes, add the milk, and then, as Devo would sing, "Whip it, whip it good." Keep it up until the potatoes are as soft and moist as you like. Add salt, pepper, and truffle oil to taste.

cook and tell

Bet his mom never drizzled truffle oil over her silky spuds. We do, and it releases an intoxicating perfume that will make him swoon.

Need extra time to work on the arch of your eyebrow? Mash the potatoes up to 1 hour in advance. Keep them warm in the top of a double boiler set over simmering water, or add an extra pat of butter and microwave them just before serving.

● Serves 2

Crunchy and salty and sensual with every bite—and that's the way we like 'em. To really make the point, eat each spear with your fingers.

Think big and long:
grilled asparagus

8 to 10 thick spears asparagus

1 tablespoon olive oil

Kosher salt and freshly ground pepper

Prepare a hot fire in a charcoal grill or preheat a gas or electric grill on high. Snap off the fibrous bottom end of each spear or trim the whole bunch to a uniform length. Peel the thick spears from slightly below the tip to the base using a vegetable peeler or sharp paring knife. In a baking dish, toss the asparagus with the olive oil and salt and pepper to taste. We like kosher salt because it has a more penetrating flavor and a distinct, coarse texture that dances on the tongue.

Lay the spears on the grill grate over the hot fire. Cover, cook for 3 minutes, and then use those tongs we told you about to turn the spears. Cover and cook for 3 minutes more, or until crisp-tender. Our advice: Some spears are thicker than others, so watch the timing or get an ego burn.

● Serves 2

cook and tell
It's a bit of a pain, but peeling asparagus gets rid of those stringy fibers (this is not the night to get one caught in your teeth). For the best texture, buck up, and peel away while humming "Love Me Tender."

Bottom-line biscuits: perfectly flaky, heady with fresh herbs, and a hint of tang—all this in 20 minutes.

I bake biscuits, too!

2 cups all-purpose flour

3/4 teaspoon kosher salt

1 teaspoon baking soda

1 tablespoon baking powder

1/4 teaspoon freshly ground pepper

4 tablespoons ice-cold unsalted butter, cut into small pieces

2 tablespoons minced fresh parsley

1 tablespoon minced fresh rosemary

3/4 cup plus 2 tablespoons buttermilk or plain yogurt

1 1/2 tablespoons olive oil for brushing

Preheat the oven to 425°F. In a large bowl, combine the dry ingredients. Scatter the butter over the top. With a pastry cutter or your fingertips, work the butter into the flour until the pieces are no larger than peas. Add the herbs and buttermilk or yogurt, stirring just to blend. (Handle the dough as little as possible to keep the biscuits tender and light.)

Turn the dough out onto a lightly floured work surface; then, with your fingertips, press into a circle about 1/2 inch thick. Cut 3-inch rounds with a biscuit cutter or the rim of a glass. Reshape any remaining dough and cut more biscuits. Place the rounds on an ungreased baking sheet. (If making ahead, cover and refrigerate until ready to pop in the oven.)

Brush the biscuits with olive oil. Bake until golden brown, about 18 to 20 minutes.

● Makes 10 to 12 biscuits

cook and tell

Of course, biscuits straight from the oven are the ideal, but get real: You've got to primp at some point. Bake early in the day and rewarm before serving. Pack up leftovers for your date to take home . . . score!!

Heaps of hot, juicy apples in a kickin' sour-cream crust. The guy already thinks he's eating in the dining room of paradise . . . and then these unexpected jolts of lemon zest and currants provide yet another surge of heavenly bliss.

Guy pie

PIE CRUST

2¹/₂ cups all-purpose flour, plus extra for dusting

1 teaspoon kosher salt

2 teaspoons sugar

¹/₂ cup (1 stick) ice-cold unsalted butter, cut into small pieces

¹/₂ cup ice-cold solid vegetable shortening

¹/₃ cup sour cream

2 tablespoons ice water

FILLING

¹/₃ cup dried currants

8 large, slightly underripe Golden Delicious apples

Zest of 1 lemon, minced

2 tablespoons fresh lemon juice

¹/₂ cup each: granulated sugar and packed brown sugar

¹/₄ teaspoon freshly grated nutmeg

1¹/₂ teaspoons ground cinnamon

¹/₂ teaspoon kosher salt

3 tablespoons all-purpose flour

2 tablespoons unsalted butter, cut into small pieces

2 tablespoons milk

1 tablespoon turbinado sugar or granulated sugar

To make the crust: If you suffer from pie-making phobia, we're here to help. This crust is forgiving and foolproof. Trust us—if you style your hair, you can handle this. Combine the flour, salt, and sugar in a food processor fitted with the metal blade. Add the butter and shortening. Pulse until the mixture resembles coarse meal. Add the sour cream and ice water. Process for a few seconds, just until a ball of dough begins to form. Do not overprocess. Transfer to a floured work surface, gathering all the loose bits, and form into a disk about 1 inch thick. Cut into 2 pieces, wrap each one in plastic wrap, and refrigerate 30 minutes, or overnight. Bada-bing. You're halfway there.

To make the filling: Place the currants in a small bowl and cover with hot water. Peel and core the apples. Cut into $1/2$-inch-thick slices. Toss them in a large bowl with the lemon zest and juice, the sugars, nutmeg, cinnamon, salt, and flour. Drain the currants and add them to the apple mixture. Set aside.

To assemble: Position a rack in the center of the oven and place another rack under it. Preheat the oven to 400°F. Have a 10-inch pie pan ready. On a lightly floured work surface, roll out one piece of dough into a 12-inch circle. This is where the scary part comes in: the Big Transfer. Roll the dough around the rolling pin (think of the way you roll your hair around a curler). Then, simply lift and center it over the pan. Now all you have to do is unroll it. If it's off-center, lift and move it. If it tears, pinch it together—it will have that, er, homemade charm. Gently press in place, leaving a 1-inch overhang

cook and tell
Turbinado sugar, a large-crystal sugar found at supermarkets, has it all over granulated sugar as a seductively crunchy finishing touch.

Roll out the remaining piece of dough into a 12-inch circle. Spoon the filling into the pie shell, mounding it in the center. Scatter the butter over the apples. Then, a nifty move: Using a pastry brush dipped in the milk, moisten the edge of the bottom crust—the milk is the "glue" that holds the top and bottom together. Drape the top crust over the pie. Lightly press the top and bottom crust edges together, trimming any excess dough with a knife. Crimp the edges. Cut 3 or 4 slits in the top crust. Brush with more milk, and sprinkle with the sugar.

Place the pie in the center of the oven, and place a rimmed baking sheet on the rack below to catch pie drips. Bake until the crust is golden brown, about 50 minutes. Cool on a rack. Serve warm or at room temperature.

● Makes one 10-inch pie

6

Bonfire of the
miseries

Welcome back to bachelorettehood

Who says breaking up is hard to do? A relationship that went sour never tasted so sweet as when your best girlfriends have gathered around a bonfire of old photographs and letters, while a ritual roast of your ex sizzles on the grill. Nothing resurrects the spirits of love lost better than watching the flames engulf a banana while you stab another pair of melon balls with your needle-sharp skewers. Rake the bozo (slowly) over the coals with a chile-blasted, rum-soaked pork tenderloin. This is a new twist on food as therapy. As you and your friends party around the embers, remember, he probably wasn't good enough for you anyway, and he can kiss your ash good-bye.

Jerk chicken with grilled bananas

Skewered melon balls and wrathful grapes

Chauvinist pig

Can 'em

Who's sari now?

How could I be sarong?

There are two kinds of jerks in this world: One is a scorching paste born in the fiery grill pits of Jamaica; the other is the guy who slowly burns you in a searing, maddening, maybe even tasteless way. This recipe acknowledges them both, though we know who the grilled bananas are meant for.

Jerk chicken with
grilled bananas

1 chicken (4 to 4¹/₂ pounds), cut into 8 pieces

1 cup Jerk Paste (page 30)

3 tablespoons unsalted butter, melted

2 tablespoons molasses

Vegetable oil for brushing

4 to 6 firm, ripe bananas, unpeeled, halved lengthwise

cook and tell

If you need more time to cut up photos of your ex, know that jerk paste can be found at well-stocked supermarkets.

Place the chicken pieces in a 1-gallon resealable plastic bag, or in a shallow baking pan. Coat all sides of the chicken with the Jerk Paste. Seal the bag or cover the pan. Refrigerate 2 to 4 hours. Occasionally turn—make that *slam*—the bag or rotate the chicken pieces to keep the sides coated. Remove from the refrigerator 30 minutes prior to grilling.

Prepare a medium-hot fire in a charcoal grill or preheat a gas or electric grill on medium-high. In a small bowl, thoroughly combine 1 tablespoon of the butter with the molasses. Set aside.

Brush the grill grate with vegetable oil. Place the coated chicken directly over the medium-hot fire. (Burn, baby, burn.) Cover the grill and cook the chicken on one side, about 12 minutes. Turn and cover again. Cook about 12 minutes more, or until the juices run clear when pierced with a knife (straight to the heart), or an instant-read thermometer registers 165°F when inserted into the thickest part of the breast and thigh. Transfer to a platter and keep warm while you grill the bananas.

Brush the bananas with the remaining butter. Grill, cut-side down, until the bananas begin to turn golden brown —and sizzle!—about 2 minutes. Turn and grill, skin-side down, 2 minutes more. Remove from the grill and brush generously with the molasses glaze. Serve alongside the chicken while singing "I Got You, Babe."

● Serves 4 to 6

This is a simple recipe for revenge—a productive and terrifically tasty way to channel your anger when you've been treated like some leftover fruit on the tray. Go on, throw a party—and let the skewering begin.

Skewered melon balls and
wrathful grapes

1 ripe cantaloupe

1 ripe honeydew melon

1 large bunch seedless green grapes

6 paper-thin slices prosciutto, cut in half crosswise

12 (6-inch-long) bamboo skewers

1 lime, cut into 6 wedges

Cut the cantaloupe and honeydew in half and remove the seeds. With a melon baller, scoop as many balls as possible from the flesh and place each fruit in a separate bowl. Discard the rinds. Remove the stems from the grapes and place the grapes in a bowl. Roll the prosciutto into pencil-thin wraps and arrange on a plate.

Here's where the fun begins: Thrust a honeydew melon ball on a skewer, then a ball of cantaloupe, a couple of grapes, a prosciutto roll, more grapes, and finish with 2 more melon balls. Do the same with the remaining skewers. Squeeze some lime juice over the tops. Sensuously bring a skewer to your lips, pop a splendiferous melon ball or two in your mouth, and bite hard. Very hard. Enjoy every mouthful.

● Serves 6

cook and tell
Even when you're not out for revenge, this is fabulous finger food for a summer grill party.

63

Better to grill some tasty swine than to live with one. Celebrate your newfound freedom with supportive pals and pork tenderloin gone tropical with tart, chile-fueled flavors and rum-grilled pineapple. Paradise found.

Chauvinist
pig

2 pork tenderloins (about 1¹/2 to 2 pounds total), trimmed of silver skin

1 cup Jerk Paste (page 30)

3 tablespoons unsalted butter, melted

2 tablespoons sugar

3 tablespoons dark rum

¹/4 teaspoon freshly ground pepper

1 ripe pineapple, peeled, halved lengthwise, and cut crosswise into ¹/2-inch-thick slices

Vegetable oil for brushing

Place the pork in a 1-gallon resealable plastic bag or in a shallow baking pan. Coat all sides of the pork with the Jerk Paste. Seal the bag or cover the pan.

Refrigerate and marinate 2 to 4 hours. Turn the bag or the pork occasionally to coat all sides. Remove from the refrigerator 30 minutes prior to grilling.

Prepare a medium fire in a charcoal grill or preheat a gas or electric grill on medium.

While the grill is heating, combine the butter, sugar, rum, and pepper in a small bowl. Place the pineapple in a single layer on a rimmed baking sheet and brush both sides with the rum mixture. Set aside.

Brush the grill grate with vegetable oil. Place the pork directly over the medium fire. Cover the grill and cook the pork for about 6 minutes. Turn and cover again. Cook another 6 to 7 minutes, or until the meat is slightly pink in the center, or an instant-read thermometer registers 145°F when stabbed, oops, we mean inserted into the tenderloin's thickest part. Remove the tenderloins, tent with foil, and set aside.

Rake the coals together or turn the burners to high (and imagine vaporizing him with flame-throwing eyes). Arrange the pineapple slices in a single layer directly over the hot fire. Cover the grill and cook until grill marks appear, about 5 minutes. Turn the pineapple and grill until golden, about 5 minutes longer. Remove from the grill and brush with any remaining rum mixture.

Cut the pork into $1/2$-inch-thick slices, arrange on a plate, and serve with the grilled pineapple. Pig out. You earned it.

● Serves 6

cook and tell
The rum mixture also works wonders on sliced mangoes, halved nectarines, or slices of grilled sweet potatoes.

The guy version of this dish is beer-can chicken, an innocent, primitive way of vertically grill-roasting a bird. We found this barbaric technique opened a whole new world of therapy and saucy ideas for women back from the edge of heartbreak.

Can 'em

2 cups hickory or mesquite chips

1 cup barbecue sauce, preferably KC Masterpiece Original

$1/2$ cup whiskey, preferably Jack Daniels

1 whole chicken (4 to $4^1/2$ pounds), fat removed

Kosher salt and freshly ground pepper

1 can Diet Coke

Disposable foil pan

Soak the wood chips in cold water to cover for 1 hour. Set up the grill for indirect cooking (see page 20). Prepare a hot fire in a charcoal grill or preheat one side of a gas or electric grill on high.

While the grill is heating, prepare the chicken: In a small bowl, mix together the barbecue sauce and whiskey. Sprinkle the chicken inside and out with salt and pepper. Slather about $1/2$ cup of the barbecue sauce and whiskey mixture all over the bird. Set aside. Open the Diet Coke and pour about one-third of the can into an ice-filled glass and drink it. Reserve the rest in the can.

Drain the chips and sprinkle half of them over the coals, or place half in the grill's smoker box. Place a disposable foil pan under the grate (on the unlit side of the grill) to catch the drippings.

Here comes the fun part: Stand the Coke can on a work surface. What you are going to do is basically impale the chicken on the can. When you sense a homicidal rage or a smash-and-stomp moment coming on, this will feel great. Stand the chicken up and ease it over the can as you insert it into the bird's main cavity. Adjust and spread the chicken's legs to form a tripod. This stabilizes the bird so it can be grill-

roasted standing up. Carefully transfer the chicken to the side of the grill without coals under it, centering the chicken over the drip pan. Adjust the chicken's legs to stabilize it on the grill rack.

Cover the grill and smoke-cook the chicken for 40 minutes. Turn the chicken so that the side that was facing the heat is now turned away from it. Add the rest of the soaked wood chips, cover, and grill another 40 minutes. Baste the chicken with half of the remaining barbecue and whiskey sauce. Cover and cook 10 minutes. Baste the chicken again with the last of the sauce. Cover and grill another 10 minutes, or until the juices run clear when pierced with a knife, or an instant-read thermometer registers 165°F when inserted into the thickest parts of the breast and thigh.

Carefully transfer the chicken, still standing up, to a baking dish and carry it to a carving board. Lift the bird off the can and let the chicken rest for 5 minutes before carving and serving. Feeling better? He's history, and this is chicken to die for.

● Serves 4 to 6

cook and tell
Any of our Spice Girls marinades, pastes, or dry rubs (pages 24-31) would be dynamo with this bird. Or substitute one of your own favorites.

Nothing like chicken kebabs, colorfully dressed in curry spices and bejeweled with emerald cilantro leaves, to light up a summer night when you thought you'd never party again. Levitate thoughts of him to some Himalayan cave, fill your backyard with upbeat friends, and fire up the action.

Who's sari now?

2¹/₂ pounds boneless, skinless chicken thighs, cut into 1-inch pieces

¹/₂ cup **Sisters of the Revenge Indian Spice Rub (page 31)**

CUCUMBER RAITA
2 cups low-fat plain yogurt

1 small cucumber, peeled, seeded, and finely diced

²/₃ cup chopped fresh cilantro

1 teaspoon kosher salt

Freshly ground pepper to taste

12 (10-inch-long) bamboo skewers, soaked in water for 30 minutes, then drained

Vegetable oil for brushing

¹/₃ cup fresh cilantro leaves

Place the chicken in a medium bowl and coat all sides with the rub. Cover and refrigerate 2 to 4 hours, stirring occasionally to keep the chicken pieces coated. Remove from the refrigerator 30 minutes before grilling. Meanwhile, elevate your mood—spin some Ravi Shankar on the sound system.

In a medium bowl, combine the Cucumber Raita ingredients. Taste and adjust the seasonings. Cover and refrigerate. Think about tonight's exotica outfit, but please don't make like Madonna in Indian makeup with a jeweled forehead. Your friends will really be worried about you.

Prepare a hot fire in a charcoal grill or preheat a gas or electric grill on high. Thread about 7 pieces of chicken onto each skewer.

When ready to grill, brush the grill grate with vegetable oil. Place the skewers directly over the hot fire. Cover the grill and cook on one side, about 5 minutes. Turn and cover again. Cook about 6 minutes more, or until the chicken is cooked through. Serve garnished with the cilantro leaves. Pass the raita on the side.

cook and tell

Ever wondered how to give skewered chicken that moist, melt-in-the-mouth texture? Use dark meat instead of breast meat.

● Serves 6

68

Self-loathing isn't a cure for the post-breakup blues. Feeding your soul—and exciting your taste buds—makes much more sense. These lip-singeing Indonesian chicken wings soar with lemongrass, lime juice, and lots of ginger. Go. Fly high.

How could I be
sarong?

24 chicken wings (about 4 pounds)

1¹/₂ cups Burning Desire: An Indonesian Blend (page 29)

Vegetable oil for brushing

¹/₃ cup fresh cilantro leaves

2 limes, quartered

Place the chicken wings in a 1¹/₂-gallon resealable plastic bag, or in a large bowl. Coat all sides of the chicken wings with the paste. Seal the bag or cover the bowl. Refrigerate 4 to 6 hours. Turn the bag or stir the wings occasionally to coat all sides.

Prepare a medium fire in a charcoal grill or preheat a gas or electric grill on medium. Brush the grill grate with vegetable oil.

Place the coated chicken wings directly over the medium fire. Cover the grill and cook on one side, about 12 minutes. Turn and cover again. Grill about 12 minutes more, or until the juices run clear when pierced with a knife. Serve on a platter garnished with the cilantro and lime wedges (for squeezing on top). Serve immediately or keep warm.

● Serves 6

cook and tell

These wings keep and travel well. Take them to the beach, on a picnic, or to a potluck. If you-know-who is on the guest list, just think, "Eat your heart out—you'll never eat these wings in this town again."

7

Sassy
sides

In the real world, side dishes are rarely invited to the party. They're the Cinderellas of the culinary universe—dressed down, waiting to be discovered, but full of beautiful secrets. Here, they've been spiffed up, cut loose, unhinged: You'll find exotic couplings; coleslaw from another galaxy; roasted potato salad with the crisp, salty snap of superior French fries; and juicy grilled pears spilling fermented nectar. So, kiss baked potatoes good-bye. And remember: None of these dishes lose their luster at midnight. Some even taste better.

You goat, girl

Undressed

The skinny on coleslaw

Real girls eat their vegetables

Currant affairs: Grilled pears and Cognac

Grilled corn with hot lips chili butter

Mrs. Potato Head salad

Consider this a still life: crisp-tender green beans, voluptuous grilled figs, and toasted walnuts slicked with nut oil. Arrange with crumbles of creamy-white goat cheese that spill over a field of garden hues.

You *goat,*

DRESSING

1/3 cup walnut oil

2 tablespoons rice wine vinegar

1 teaspoon sugar

1/2 teaspoon kosher salt

1 tablespoon minced shallot

Freshly ground pepper to taste

1 tablespoon plus 1/4 teaspoon kosher salt

1 pound young, tender green beans, trimmed

1/2 cup chopped walnuts

2 teaspoons walnut oil

12 ripe black Mission figs, halved

Vegetable oil for brushing

3 ounces goat cheese

To make the dressing: In a jar with a tight-fitting lid, combine the dressing ingredients. Shake well, making sure the sugar dissolves. Set aside.

Fill a large stockpot three-quarters full with water, cover, and bring to a boil. Have ready a large bowl of ice water. Add the 1 tablespoon salt to the boiling water, then the beans, and cook until bright green and crisp-tender, 2 to 4 minutes. Drain the beans and plunge into the ice water until cold, about 1 to 2 minutes. Drain, wrap in several layers of paper towels, and place in a plastic bag. Refrigerate until 30 minutes before serving.

Meanwhile, preheat the oven to 325°F. Toss the walnuts with the remaining 1/4 teaspoon salt and the walnut oil. Spread on a rimmed baking sheet and bake until lightly browned, about 8 to 10 minutes. Set aside.

Prepare a medium fire in a charcoal grill or preheat a gas or electric grill on medium.

girl

Brush the figs with vegetable oil. When ready to grill, brush the grill grate with vegetable oil. Place the figs directly over the medium fire. Grill, cut-side down, just until grill marks appear, about 1 minute. Turn and grill until tender but still firm, about 1 minute.

Place the beans and figs in a large bowl and toss with the dressing. Divide among individual salad plates. Garnish with the walnuts and crumble some goat cheese on top.

● Serves 6

cook and tell

Walnut oil adds an unctuous, nutty-rich flavor to salads. Be sure to refrigerate after opening. Delicate Japanese rice wine vinegar balances this dish perfectly.

The heart of summer on a plate: the ripest toma-
toes, sliced and intertwined with fresh mozzarella,
basil leaves, and drizzles of olive oil — just naked,
elegant simplicity.

Undressed

1/2 cup loosely packed fresh basil leaves

2 pounds ripe red and yellow tomatoes, preferably heirloom varieties, sliced 1/4 inch thick

1 pound fresh mozzarella, sliced 1/4 inch thick

1/4 cup extra-virgin olive oil

Kosher salt and freshly ground pepper

Make a stack of 6 of the basil leaves and slice them crosswise into thin slivers. Set aside.

Now the fun part: color coordinating and putting that urge to decorate to good use. On a serving platter, alternate slices of tomato and mozzarella, overlapping them and slipping a whole basil leaf between each. Scatter the slivered basil over the top. No rules here, really. Cut loose with your own slice-and-dice arrangement.

Drizzle the salad with the olive oil. Season to taste with salt and pepper. Serve with plenty of good crusty bread to mop up the juices.

● Serves 4

cook and tell

This is a place where virginity is worth keeping. For salads, extra-virgin olive oil is like a good wine: distinctive and mouth filling, with a long, smooth finish.

This is not your mother's coleslaw. We're twistin' on the tropics here, with papaya, curry, and mint, plus a little chili to get your attention. The final production is light, crunchy, and full of pucker power.

The skinny
on coleslaw

1 small head green cabbage (about 1¹/2 pounds), halved, cored, and sliced into thin shreds

2 ripe papayas, peeled, halved, seeded, and cut into ¹/2-inch dice

DRESSING
Zest of 1 lemon

¹/3 cup fresh lemon juice

²/3 cup olive oil

1 tablespoon kosher salt

1 tablespoon sugar

1 teaspoon chili powder

1 teaspoon curry powder

¹/4 cup coarsely chopped fresh mint leaves

Freshly ground pepper to taste

In a large bowl, combine the cabbage and papaya. Cover and refrigerate.

In a jar with a tight-fitting lid, combine the dressing ingredients. Imagine some hot rumba beat and shake the ingredients like a wild night on a forbidden beach. (OK, you can stop now.) Taste and adjust the seasonings. Set aside.

One hour before serving, shake the dressing well and pour over the cabbage-papaya mixture. Toss until thoroughly combined. Serve at room temperature.

● Serves 6 to 8

cook and tell
The cure for the common coleslaw: Keep the cabbage crisp by not dressing it too far in advance.

75

Vegetables belong in the real girls' Top Four food groups, along with chocolate chip cookies, ice cream, and fat-free crackers. And they're never better than hot off the grill, especially with a dab of garlicky basil oil.

Real girls
eat their vegetables

2 medium zucchini, sliced diagonally into 1/4-inch-thick ovals

2 medium summer squash, sliced diagonally into 1/4-inch-thick ovals

3 Japanese eggplants, sliced in half lengthwise

1 large sweet onion, sliced into 1/4-inch-thick rounds

1 sweet red bell pepper, quartered, seeded, and deribbed

1 sweet yellow bell pepper, quartered, seeded, and deribbed

1/2 cup olive oil

Kosher salt and freshly ground pepper

PESTO OIL (OPTIONAL)
3 tablespoons olive oil

1/4 cup store-bought pesto, at room temperature

Vegetable oil for brushing

Prepare a hot fire in a charcoal grill or preheat a gas or electric grill on high. Lay the vegetables in a single layer on a rimmed baking sheet. Brush on both sides with the 1/2 cup olive oil. Sprinkle salt and pepper on the top side of each vegetable.

If you are using the Pesto Oil, in a small bowl, combine the 3 tablespoons olive oil with the pesto. Set aside.

When ready to grill, brush the grill grate with vegetable oil. Place the vegetables in a single layer directly over the hot fire. Grill, cut-side down, just until grill marks appear, about 3 minutes. Turn and grill until tender, but still firm, about 2 to 3 minutes longer.

Serve warm, drizzled, if desired, with the Pesto Oil.

● Serves 6

cook and tell
Got leftovers? Chop and toss the vegetables with cooked pasta and additional Pesto Oil. Or, serve on crusty bread with some smoky cheese or creamy goat cheese.

Who needs baked potatoes when grilled pears, glistening with butter and topped with Cognac-soaked currants, are just a few flames away? Did we mention they are simple to make?

Currant affairs:
Grilled pears and Cognac

⅓ cup dried currants

¼ cup Cognac or another brandy

Pinch of freshly ground pepper

6 medium Anjou pears, peeled

4 tablespoons unsalted butter, melted

Vegetable oil for brushing

Prepare a hot fire in a charcoal grill or preheat a gas or electric grill on high.

In a small bowl, combine the currants, Cognac, and pepper. Macerate (which is like taking a bath in liqueur—something we all aspire to) until ready to serve.

Cut the pears in half lengthwise, and use a melon baller or paring knife to remove the core, leaving a gumball-sized hole. Place in a shallow dish and brush all over with melted butter.

When ready to grill, brush the grill grate with vegetable oil. Place the pears, cut-side up, in a single layer directly over the hot fire. Cook just until grill marks appear, about 3 minutes. Brush with any butter remaining in the dish, then turn and grill until tender but firm, about 3 to 4 minutes more.

Serve warm with a little Cognac-soaked currant sauce spooned over the top.

● Serves 6

cook and tell

To prepare the pears in advance, prep them and place in a big bowl of cold water mixed with the juice of a lemon. Drain and blot dry before brushing with the butter and grilling.

Southwestern heat infuses these crisp, smoky, grilled-in-the-husk kernels, which get even better when smeared with our lip-tingling butter.

Grilled corn with
hot lips chili butter

6 fresh ears of corn

CHILI BUTTER
4 tablespoons unsalted butter at room temperature

1/2 teaspoon chili powder

Pinch of cayenne pepper

1/4 teaspoon sugar

1/2 teaspoon kosher salt

2 tablespoons minced fresh cilantro

Vegetable oil for brushing

Prepare a hot fire in a charcoal grill or preheat a gas or electric grill on high.

Pull back the husk from each ear of corn without actually removing it. Remove the silk, then re-cover the corn with the husk. Run water into the ears of corn, drain the excess, and twist the husks at the top to close.

To make the chili butter: In a small bowl, combine the ingredients thoroughly and set aside.

When ready to grill, brush the grill grate with vegetable oil. Place the corn directly over the hot fire. Grill for about 20 minutes, turning several times to grill all sides. Remove from the grill and pull back and discard the husks, or knot them for that oh-so-rustic-chic look. Generously brush the corn with the chili butter. Serve hot.

● Serves 6

cook and tell

We call it *muy* authentic. But if you're not into the corn husk thing, just rip those babies off. Brush the corn with the chili butter, wrap the ears in foil, and grill away.

This is like some great cross between super French fries and soul food potato salad, but without the deep-fry/mayonnaise sin. Crispy, golden potatoes are strewn with a confetti of red peppers and rosemary. The flavors come in waves: big dynamos of garlic and shallots, followed by a zing of fresh lemon and the bite of coarsely ground pepper.

Mrs. Potato Head
salad

2 pounds small new potatoes, quartered

2 teaspoons kosher salt

1/3 cup olive oil

1 tablespoon minced garlic

1/4 cup minced shallots

2 teaspoons minced fresh rosemary

1/2 cup diced sweet red bell pepper

Paprika for sprinkling

Juice of 1/2 lemon

Freshly ground pepper

Preheat the oven to 375°F. Place the potatoes in a roasting pan and toss with the salt, then with the olive oil. Set the pan on a burner over medium-high heat. Cook, stirring frequently, until the potatoes are just beginning to soften, but not brown, about 10 minutes.

Transfer the pan to the oven. Bake, uncovered, 15 minutes, stirring every 5 minutes with a spatula, pushing under the potatoes each time to make sure they don't stick to the pan.

Stir in the garlic, shallots, and rosemary. Cook another 15 minutes, stirring every 5 minutes. Stir in the bell pepper and sprinkle with enough paprika to make a light coating. Bake until nicely browned, about 15 minutes longer, stirring every 5 minutes.

Remove from the oven. Cool to room temperature. Sprinkle the lemon juice over the top, add a few grinds of pepper, and serve.

● Serves 4 to 6

cook and tell

Great potatoes are all about the right amount of salt. The best test is to dip your finger in the olive oil and taste for a crackling salt intensity. If it's not there, pump up the volume.

Desperately
seeking sugar

Girls, we are nothing if not complicated. By day, we'll righteously dine on organic grapefruit juice and horrid-tasting, fat-melting miracle kelp crackers. By night, we turn into chocolate Terminators, stalking specialty food shops for the most premium species of chocolate. We hunt down that sensual taste of seasonal fruit and imagine it oozing madly out of the edges of a toasty oat crust chunked with walnuts. When we're really out of

8

Campy s'mores sundae
with toasted
marshmallows

Babelicious berries

Reason-to-live
chocolate-glazed cheesecake

Grilled peaches in a dark
rum bath

The great fruit-crisp experiment

PMS espresso-chocolate-walnut
brownies

Hot-flash key lime pie

control, we pervert an innocent Girls Scouts' campfire classic into a shameless indulgence of raw, lip-smacking pleasure. Perfect meal closers or stand-alone mood elevators—these desserts satisfy either way.

An urban girl's idea of a Girl Scout campfire dessert experience: Forage the supermarket for first-rate gelato, hunt down the best chocolate sauce, nab some marshmallows, and toast them proudly over a one-match grill fire. Troop 66 never had it so good, right down to the chocolate grahams on the side.

Campy
s'mores sundae
with toasted marshmallows

1 pint coconut gelato, preferably Häagen-Dazs

Remove the gelato from the freezer and let stand at room temperature until soft enough to run a spoon through it, about 10 to 20 minutes. Transfer the gelato to a medium bowl. Stir in the chopped chocolate. Repack the gelato into the carton. Freeze for several hours or overnight.

1/3 cup coarsely chopped bittersweet chocolate

12 marshmallows

Prepare a hot fire in a charcoal grill or preheat a gas or electric grill on high. Thread 3 marshmallows onto each skewer. This is the bonding moment. Give each pal her own skewer, stand around and giggle, and pledge to cook the marshmallows until puffed and toasty-brown, turning as needed. Cook the marshmallows and hand out badges.

4 metal skewers

8 ounces good-quality chocolate sauce, warmed

4 chocolate graham crackers

To assemble: Place 1 scoop of gelato in each of 4 dessert bowls. Drizzle approximately 2 tablespoons of the chocolate sauce over each scoop. Top each serving with 3 toasted marshmallows. Serve immediately with a graham cracker on the side.

● Serves 4

cook and tell

Despite what Mom said, never miss an opportunity to play with food. Try other ice-cream fantasies. Vanilla ice cream with crushed Girl Scout mint cookies, anyone?

Strawberries marinated in balsamic vinegar and sugar are as deeply rich and mellow as a good Port. Mascarpone cheese adds the sexy-sweet finish that lingers on the tongue. Chic and easy.

Babelicious
berries

2 pints fresh strawberries

1/4 cup light brown sugar

2 to 4 tablespoons balsamic vinegar

8 ounces mascarpone cheese

Stem and halve the strawberries. In a large bowl, toss the strawberries with the sugar and vinegar to taste. Let macerate for 30 minutes. Serve with dollops of mascarpone cheese.

● Serves 6

cook and tell

There's an art to choosing great-tasting strawberries: Look for berries that are red, not white, at the stem and have an unmistakable strawberry aroma. Best test: Ask for a taste.

Chocolate, chocolate, and more chocolate. If there's a better reason for living, we haven't found it. Not even Russell Crowe (well . . . maybe). Resist the urge to sneak a quick slice—this is best made a day ahead if you want that luxuriously creamy texture.

Reason-to-live chocolate-glazed cheesecake

CRUST

6 tablespoons unsalted butter, melted

2 cups chocolate wafer crumbs (about 7 ounces of cookies)

1¹/₂ tablespoons sugar

Pinch of salt

2 teaspoons ground cinnamon

GLAZE

6 ounces bittersweet chocolate, finely chopped

2 tablespoons heavy (whipping) cream

FILLING

8 ounces bittersweet chocolate, finely chopped

2 tablespoons heavy (whipping) cream

3 packages (8 ounces each) cream cheese, softened

1 cup sugar

2 large eggs, lightly beaten

1¹/₂ teaspoons pure vanilla extract

1 tablespoon ground cinnamon

¹/₃ cup double-strength espresso, cooled

1 cup sour cream

To make the crust: Preheat the oven to 350°F. Butter a 9- or 10-inch springform pan with 1 tablespoon of the melted butter. In a medium bowl, combine the chocolate wafer crumbs, sugar, salt, and cinnamon. Blend in the remaining butter. Press the crumbs into the bottom and about 1¹/₂ inches up the sides of the pan. Bake until crisp, about 8 to 10 minutes. Transfer to a cooling rack.

To make the filling: Fill a medium saucepan one-third full with water and bring to a simmer. Place the chocolate and heavy cream in a heat-proof medium bowl set over the simmering water. Turn off the heat. Melt the chocolate completely, stirring frequently. Set aside.

In a food processor fitted with the metal blade (or using an electric mixer), process the cream cheese until smooth. Mix in the sugar, then the eggs, and process until thoroughly combined, scraping down the sides of the bowl once or twice. Add the vanilla, cinnamon, espresso, melted chocolate, and sour cream. Process until completely smooth and well combined. (Alternatively, using an electric mixer, add and mix the ingredients in the same order.)

Gently pour the filling into the crust. It's OK if the filling rises above it. Place the cheesecake in the center of the oven and bake until the sides are slightly puffed, about 40 to 50 minutes. The center of the filling will be very soft and will jiggle when you shake the pan gently. Turn off the oven and leave the cheesecake inside for 20 minutes. Transfer to a rack and cool in the pan. Cover and refrigerate at least 6 hours, but preferably overnight.

One or two hours before serving, make the glaze: Place the chocolate in a heat-proof medium bowl. Bring the heavy cream to a boil in a small saucepan. Pour the hot cream over the chocolate and stir until completely smooth. Cool slightly. Remove the cheesecake from the refrigerator, unlatch and remove the rim of the pan, and carefully transfer the cake to a cake plate. Use paper towels to blot any moisture from the top of the cheesecake. Gently pour the glaze onto center of the cake, and use a long, narrow spatula to spread it evenly over the top. Refrigerate until ready to serve.

cook and tell

No espresso maker? Instant espresso powder to the rescue. Just make it double strength and you're wired.

To serve, cut slices with a warm, wet knife, wiping the knife clean between slices.

● Serves 10 to 12

Peach halves splashed in the quintessential tropical tonic—rum, butter, and dark sugar—and grilled to juicy perfection. Things really get lusty when the warm fruit encounters a cold blast of caramel ice cream.

Grilled peaches
in a dark rum bath

1 tablespoon unsalted butter

2 tablespoons dark brown sugar

¹/₄ cup dark rum

6 ripe peaches, halved and pitted

1 pint caramel ice cream

Prepare a medium fire in a charcoal grill or preheat a gas or electric grill on medium.

In a small saucepan set over low heat, melt the butter. Remove from the heat and add the brown sugar and rum. Stir until the sugar dissolves. (Cleanup avoidance alert: Use a microwave and melt the butter in a little bowl that can be thrown in the dishwasher.)

Place the peach halves in a large bowl. With a rubber spatula, gently stir in the rum mixture and continue stirring until the peaches are well coated.

Grill the peaches directly over the medium fire; cut-side up, until grill marks are visible, about 5 minutes. Turn the peaches over. Cook until grill marks show and the peaches are tender, about 4 or 5 minutes more.

Instead of licking the bowl, brush any leftover rum mixture on the peaches as they grill.

Serve warm with a scoop of ice cream.

● Serves 6

cook and tell

Keep a stash of amaretti cookies on hand. Crush a few over the top for some amazing mouth crunch.

A mound of hot fruit bubbling and oozing under a nutty oat topping is our idea of the perfect crisp. You get to play with the fruit flavors. Mix and match away; just make sure it all adds up to 6 cups. How about half cherries and half apricots; or an explosion of strawberries, blackberries, and blues; or a density of peaches scattered with raspberries?

The great fruit-crisp experiment

TOPPING
1/3 cup chopped walnuts

2/3 cup each: old-fashioned oats and all-purpose flour

1/3 cup packed light brown sugar

3/4 teaspoon cinnamon

1/2 teaspoon freshly grated nutmeg

4 tablespoons ice-cold unsalted butter, cut into small pieces

FILLING (OUR PERSONAL FAVE)
5 cups sliced nectarines (about 6 large nectarines)

1 cup (1/2 pint) fresh blueberries

1/2 cup sugar

2 tablespoons all-purpose flour

3 tablespoons orange juice

To make the topping: Preheat the oven to 375°F. Spread the walnuts on a rimmed baking sheet and toast in the oven until lightly browned, about 6 minutes. Set aside. In a medium bowl, combine the oats, flour, sugar, cinnamon, and nutmeg. Scatter the butter over the top. Using your fingertips, blend the butter into the flour mixture until the mixture is crumbly. Add the nuts and mix well.

To make the filling: In a large bowl, combine the nectarines and blueberries. In a small bowl, blend the sugar, flour, and orange juice until the sugar and flour are dissolved. Add to the fruit, stirring gently to blend. Spoon into a 1 1/2-quart baking dish.

Sprinkle the topping evenly over the fruit, pressing down lightly. Bake until the top is nicely browned and the fruit is tender when pierced with a fork, about 30 to 40 minutes. Serve warm. Vanilla ice cream or frozen yogurt ups the bliss factor.

● Serves 6

cook and tell
One of the seven habits of highly organized baking mavens: Double, triple, even quadruple the topping and freeze it. Next time you want to make a crisp, measure out 2 cups of the topping. Bake away and feel smug.

Light, gooey, and very chocolaty, with just the right amount of buzz to counter a monthly mood attack. On the bodacious brownie scale, a 10!

PMS espresso-chocolate-walnut brownies

Vegetable-oil cooking spray

3/4 cup chopped walnuts

1 cup cake flour, or 3/4 cup all-purpose flour

1/4 cup unsweetened cocoa powder

1/4 teaspoon kosher salt

3/4 teaspoon baking powder

1 1/2 tablespoons finely ground espresso beans

3 ounces unsweetened chocolate, finely chopped

3/4 cup (1 1/2 sticks) unsalted butter at room temperature

1 1/2 cups sugar

3 large eggs, lightly beaten

1 teaspoon vanilla extract

Preheat the oven to 350°F. Spray an 8-by-8-inch baking dish with cooking spray. Line the pan with aluminum foil; then spray the foil with cooking spray.

Spread the walnuts on a rimmed baking sheet and toast in the oven until lightly browned, about 6 to 8 minutes. Set aside to cool.

Meanwhile, sift together the flour, cocoa powder, salt, and baking powder into a small bowl. Stir in the ground espresso and set aside.

Fill a medium saucepan one-third full with water and bring to a simmer. Place the chocolate and butter in a large heat-proof bowl and set over the simmering water. Turn the heat to low. Melt the chocolate and butter, stirring frequently, until completely smooth. Remove from heat and stir in the sugar. Whisk in the eggs and vanilla. Stir in the flour mixture just until the flour is absorbed. Stir in the nuts.

Pour the batter evenly into the pan. Bake until a crust forms on top and the center is still somewhat gooey, but not *Baywatch* jiggly, about 30 to 35 minutes. Cool in the pan set on a rack. Refrigerate 2 hours. Cut into 1-inch squares to serve.

● Makes 64 bite-size brownies

cook and tell

Keep those extra brownies in the freezer. As the crabby mood kicks in, pop one of these trufflelike gems. Better than Motrin, and twice the fun.

The mythical Florida Keys pie just as it was meant to be: a tart, creamy custard dotted with lime zest in a cinnamon-perfumed crust, all topped with billowing whipped cream.

Hot-flash
key lime pie

CRUST

1¹/2 cups graham cracker crumbs

2 tablespoons sugar

1 teaspoon ground cinnamon

6 tablespoons unsalted butter, melted

FILLING

6 large egg yolks, lightly beaten

2 cans (14 ounces each) sweetened condensed milk

1 tablespoon lime zest

1 cup fresh key lime juice, or ¹/2 cup fresh lime juice plus ¹/2 cup fresh lemon juice

TOPPING

1 teaspoon cornstarch

2 tablespoons confectioners' sugar

1 cup heavy (whipping) cream

To make the crust: Preheat the oven to 375°F. In a medium bowl, thoroughly combine the graham cracker crumbs, sugar, cinnamon, and melted butter. Firmly press the crumbs into the bottom and up the sides of a 10-inch pie plate. Bake until crisp, about 10 to 12 minutes. Cool on a rack. Leave the oven on.

To make the filling: In a medium bowl, combine the beaten eggs yolks with the condensed milk and lime zest. Stir in the lime juice, a little at a time, until well blended. Pour the filling into the crust. Bake until it just begins to set, about 15 minutes. Remove and cool on a rack 20 minutes. Refrigerate until set, at least 2 hours.

To make the topping: In a small saucepan or microwave-safe dish combine the cornstarch and confectioners' sugar. Add ¹/4 cup of heavy cream and mix well. Cook over low heat just until thickened, or microwave on high for 20 seconds. Stir thoroughly. Let cool 5 minutes. Combine with the remaining ³/4 cup cream in the bowl of an electric mixer. Beat until soft peaks form. Cover and chill thoroughly.

Cover the pie with the whipped cream, spreading it to the edges. With a long, narrow spatula, swirl the cream to decorate.

cook and tell

They can't make perfect silk stockings, but you can make whipped cream that won't run. Just remember to add cornstarch.

● Serves 8 to 10

Liquid assets

Every girl's summer party repertoire should include the Grill Girl
High Five — an offbeat lemonade,
a dangerous daiquiri, a signature
margarita, an exotic iced tea, and
an electrifying punch that gets the
place boppin'— plus one kickin'
Champagne combo. Go as wild or
mild as the mood dictates; just
be sure to balance cocktails with
options from the alcohol-free zone.
Drinks are conversation starters,

La femme Margarita

Party Punch

Lemonade

Flaming lips
  party punch

Electric lady
  blackberry
  lemonade

La femme margarita

The Tao of mint tea

Pimm's chic-o-matic
  Champagne cooler

What women want: An
  irresistible nectarine daiquiri

9

especially if they look like art. We offer suggestions here, but open your own gallery by toying with ingredients, glass shapes, and garnishes. After a few nectarine daiquiris, you're bound to make a good impressionist.

Cocktail cooler

Mint tea

nectarine Daiquiri

Paint the toes, red-dress the lips, and get some tiki rhythm in those hips. Then whip up a batch of this passionate punch, a playful tropical elixir with a modern edge and colors as vibrant as an island sunset.

Flaming lips

party punch

6 ounces gold rum

4 ounces dark rum

5 ounces fresh orange juice

6 ounces pineapple juice

6 ounces passion fruit juice

2 ounces fresh lime juice

1 ounce grenadine

2 trays of ice cubes

GARNISH
6 orange wedges

6 pineapple wedges

6 lime wedges

In a large pitcher, combine all the ingredients except the ice and garnishes. Refrigerate until ready to serve.

Fill 6 tall glasses with ice and divide the mixture evenly among the glasses. With each of 6 cocktail picks, skewer an orange wedge between a pineapple wedge and a lime wedge. Garnish each glass and serve immediately.

● Serves 6

blend and tell

Shake it up, baby. Replace the pineapple juice with guava, mango, papaya, or other tropical juices. If you're really flying, add a few scoops of sorbet, such as lime, passion fruit, or coconut.

As deep pink as a berry smoothie, this drink is zapped with honey, lemon, and bubbles of orange intensity. Pucker up, babe.

Electric lady
blackberry lemonade

1¹/₂ cups fresh or frozen blackberries

6 ounces fresh lemon juice

2 ounces fresh orange juice

¹/₄ cup honey

16 ounces sparkling orange juice beverage, such as San Pellegrino Orangina

2 trays of ice cubes

GARNISH
6 orange wedges

6 blackberries

In a blender, whirl together the blackberries, lemon juice, orange juice, and honey until smooth.

Strain the mixture through a fine-mesh strainer into a large glass pitcher. Chill until ready to serve. Instead of wiping your fingers, smoosh any leftover blackberry mixture on your face to make a facial mask. Retire to the bathroom and lounge. You won't need to wear rouge . . . perhaps ever again.

When ready to serve, add the sparkling orange beverage to the pitcher and stir to combine.

Serve the lemonade in tall glasses filled with ice. Garnish each glass with a wedge of orange and a blackberry skewered on a cocktail pick.

● Serves 6

Blend and tell

Girlfriends, it's time to have a serious talk about ice cubes. Using tap water in ice trays is tantamount to using lard in a buttercream. Filtered or bottled water is the only the way to go, pure and simple.

For the meloncholy baby. The margarita takes off in a new direction with a peachy hue, a voluptuous melon flavor, and the perfume of lemons to mellow the traditional tartness of limes. Standing in for the usual Triple Sec is the more intriguing Tuaca, an Italian brandy infused with the aura of vanilla-orange ambrosia.

La femme

margarita

1 cup cubed cantaloupe

1 cup cubed honey-dew melon

6 ounces silver tequila

3 ounces Tuaca

3 ounces fresh lemon juice

3 ounces fresh lime juice

3 tablespoons superfine sugar

1¹/₂ cups cracked ice

GARNISH
12 melon balls

While you're chillin', chill 4 margarita or large cocktail glasses until ready to use.

In a blender, whirl the melons until puréed. Add the tequila, Tuaca, lemon juice, lime juice, sugar, and ice, blending until well combined and slushy.

Divide the mixture evenly among the chilled glasses. Garnish each glass with 3 melon balls skewered on a cocktail pick.

● Serves 4

blend and tell

To salt or not to salt . . . that is the question. This version tastes best without a salt rim. But a sugar-salt rim is a nifty alternative. Mix equal portions of superfine sugar and kosher salt on a plate. Moisten the glass rims with lime, then dip the rims into the mixture; shake off any excess.

Summer mint tea gets a makeover with orange zest, pink grapefruit juice (yes, we know it sounds a little unusual), and a kick of cloves for, well, just call it a Moroccan thing. Trust us: This tea is distinctive, refreshing, and totally enlightening.

The Tao
of mint tea

4 cups water

In a tea kettle, bring the water to a boil.

4 peppermint tea bags

2 orange pekoe tea bags

In a large teapot, place the tea bags, orange zest, mint leaves, and cloves. Pour the boiling water on top. Add the sugar and stir until dissolved. Cover and let steep until cool, about 30 to 40 minutes.

Zest of 1 orange

8 fresh mint leaves

Strain the steeped tea through a fine-mesh strainer into a large pitcher. Stir in the grapefruit juice. Serve over ice in tall glasses. Garnish with the mint sprigs.

6 whole cloves

● Serves 4 to 6

¼ cup superfine sugar

6 ounces fresh pink grapefruit juice

2 trays of ice cubes

GARNISH
4 to 6 fresh mint sprigs

blend and tell

There's no excuse for not having a zesting tool. They're inexpensive, so splurge away (nothing ever stopped you before). Zesters work miracles, turning citrus peels into art—in seconds. Get thee to a kitchen store.

This garden-party drink, created by cocktail highness Mittie Hellmich, is a modern hybrid of two retro classics: the Pimm's Cups—a prim, fruity, gin-based liqueur typically mixed with lemonade—and the Champagne cocktail, which is always good for that instant Audrey Hepburn swagger. Get out your big black sunglasses and head for the hedges.

Pimm's chic-o-matic
Champagne cooler

1/4 cup superfine sugar

1 cup peeled, cubed, cucumber

3 ounces fresh lemon juice

3 ounces fresh lime juice

6 ounces Pimm's No. 1

6 ounces chilled citrus vodka

10 ounces chilled Champagne

2 cups cracked ice or a tray of ice cubes, plus extra ice to fill glasses

GARNISH
6 thin cucumber rounds or lemon slices

In a blender, combine the sugar, cucumber, lemon juice, and lime juice until smooth. Pour into a large (1½ liter) glass pitcher. Add the Pimm's liqueur, vodka, Champagne, and the 2 cups of ice, slowly stirring to combine.

Pour the mixture into 6 tall glasses filled with ice. Cut a slit into each cucumber round or lemon slice and slide one on each rim to garnish.

● Serves 6

blend and tell
To maintain the carbonated efferves-cence, use a glass or plastic pitcher plus a glass stirring rod or a wooden spoon for stirring. Metal will dissipate the bubbles and deflate your hostess ego.

*Better shaved than peaches, more succulent
than mangoes, and sexier than Mel Gibson.
Lots of lime. Sweet rum. So divine.*

What women want:
An irresistible
nectarine daiquiri

3 cups peeled, pitted,
and cubed nectarines
(about 5 medium
nectarines)

6 ounces silver rum

3 ounces fresh lime
juice

3 tablespoons
superfine sugar

2 cups cracked ice

GARNISH
4 slices lime

Chill 4 large cocktail glasses until ready to use.

In a blender, whirl together the nectarines, rum,
lime juice, and sugar until the nectarines are
puréed and the mixture is smooth. Add the ice
and blend on high until slushy.

Divide evenly among
the glasses. Garnish
each glass with a
slice of lime.

● Serves 4

blend and tell
Forget the money you
wasted on the high-
tech juicer and do as
the Cubans do:
Squeeze the limes
with your fingers to
release the potent oils
from the rind—the key
to unleashing that
elusive daiquiri bite.

Move over, Martha

Entertaining without stenciling your napkins

Need a little help planning those parties?
Worried about what goes with what? Here
are some menu ideas. Consider us your
personal party planners.

menu 1
Girls' bonding weekend

What women want:
An irresistible nectarine daiquiri

Ragin' hormones-free chicken

The skinny on coleslaw

Grilled corn with hot lips chili butter

Campy s'mores sundae with toasted marshmallows

menu 2
Ladies who brunch

La femme margarita

Svelte salmon with fig balsamic sauce

Think big and long: grilled asparagus

Undressed (tomatoes, basil, and mozzarella)

Hot-flash key lime pie

party planner

menu 3
Vegetarian bliss

The Tao of mint tea

When penne met portobella

You goat, girl

Real girls eat their vegetables

Grilled peaches in a dark rum bath

menu 4
The fabulous finger foods fete

Electric lady blackberry lemonade

Forget Caesar: A bang-up Cleopatra salad

What a back (ribs in hoisin-ginger glaze)

How could I be sarong? (Indonesian chicken wings)

Skewered melon balls and wrathful grapes

PMS Espresso-chocolate-walnut brownies

menu 5
Dumped and out for revenge

Rum on the rocks

Jerk chicken with grilled bananas

The skinny on coleslaw

Reason-to-live chocolate-glazed cheesecake

menu 6
Love at first bite:
Six singles feast and flirt

Flaming lips party punch

Great legs (garlicky leg of lamb)

Mrs. Potato Head salad

Undressed (tomatoes, basil, and mozzarella)

Babelicious berries

Chocolate condoms

menu 7
Everybody's feeling fat
and on a diet dinner

Diet Coke

Sparkling water with lime wedges

Calorie-busting gazpacho with seared scallops

Waistland salad

Skewered melon balls and wrathful grapes

One Junior Mint each

notes

notes

notes

notes

index

Ahi Tuna: Raw, Raw, Sizzlin', Boom Bah, 40

Animal Magnetism: The Steak and the Sizzle, 54

Babelicious Berries, 83

Better Than His Mom's Mashed Potatoes, 55

Boy Toy Martini, 52

Burning Desire: An Indonesian Blend, 29

Calorie-Busting Gazpacho with Seared Scallops, 34

Campy S'mores Sundae with Toasted Marshmallows, 82

Can 'Em, 66

Chauvinist Pig, 64

Currant Affairs: Grilled Pears and Cognac, 77

Electric Lady Blackberry Lemonade, 93

Firm Thighs, 47

Flaming Lips Party Punch, 92

Forbidden Nights Moroccan Pesto, 27

Forget Caesar: A Bang-Up Cleopatra Salad, 38

Getting Naked, 46

Great Fruit-Crisp Experiment, The, 87

Great Legs, 48

Grilled Corn with Hot Lips Chili Butter, 78

Grilled Halibut with Mambo Queens Mango Salsa, 41

Grilled Peaches in a Dark Rum Bath, 86

Guy Pie, 58

Hey, I Bake Biscuits, Too!, 57

Hidden Pleasures Hoisin-Ginger Glaze, 26

Hot-Flash Key Lime Pie, 89

Hot Girls Spice Rub, 28

How Could I Be Sarong?, 69

Jerk Chicken with Grilled Bananas, 62

Jerk Paste, 30

La Femme Margarita, 94

Lemonology: A Theory of Vital Ingredients, 24

Mod Bods Mustard Marinade, 25

Mrs. Potato Head Salad, 79

Pimm's Chic-o-Matic Champagne Cooler, 96

PMS Espresso-Chocolate-Walnut Brownies, 88

Ragin' Hormones-Free Chicken, 42

Real Girls Eat Their Vegetables, 76

Reason-to-Live Chocolate-Glazed Cheesecake, 84

Sisters of the Revenge Indian Spice Rub, 31

Skewered Melon Balls and Wrathful Grapes, 63

Skinny on Coleslaw, The, 75

Svelte Salmon with Fig Balsamic Sauce, 37

Tao of Mint Tea, The, 95

Think Big and Long: Grilled Asparagus, 56

Undressed, 74

Waistland Salad, 36

What a Back, 49

What Women Want: An Irresistible Nectarine Daiquiri, 97

When Penne Met Portobella, 43

Who's Sari Now?, 68

You Goat, Girl, 72

table of equivalents

The exact equivalents in the following tables have been rounded for convenience.

LIQUID/DRY MEASURES

U.S.	METRIC
1/4 teaspoon	1.25 milliliters
1/2 teaspoon	2.5 milliliters
1 teaspoon	5 milliliters
1 tablespoon (3 teaspoons)	15 milliliters
1 fluid ounce (2 tablespoons)	30 milliliters
1/4 cup	60 milliliters
1/3 cup	80 milliliters
1/2 cup	120 milliliters
1 cup	240 milliliters
1 pint (2 cups)	480 milliliters
1 quart (4 cups, 32 ounces)	960 milliliters
1 gallon (4 quarts)	3.84 liters
1 ounce (by weight)	28 grams
1 pound	454 grams
2.2 pounds	1 kilogram

OVEN TEMPERATURES

Fahrenheit	Celsius	Gas
250	120	1/2
275	140	1
300	150	2
325	160	3
350	180	4
375	190	5
400	200	6
425	220	7
450	230	8
475	240	9
500	260	10

LENGTH

U.S.	METRIC
1/8 inch	3 millimeters
1/4 inch	6 millimeters
1/2 inch	12 millimeters
1 inch	2.5 centimeters

acknowledgments

Our grills lit up the night with the glow of experiments slicked with mad spice combos and funky-chic girlitude. For months, we pondered the male barbecue mystique and tried to figure out why guys don't just quickly grill up some nice fish, have a cosmopolitan, unload every intimate detail of their lives, and call it a great night like we do. Hopefully, with the gracious help of our friends and families, this book provides a few delicious insights. For our beloved editor and friend Bill LeBlond, his savvy assistant Amy Treadwell, and meticulous copy editor Deborah Kops, we offer a sacrificial lipstick to the grill. And to Marti and Morgan Kuhr, our supreme recipe testers, thanks for tending the flames.

KAREN BROOKS THANKS:
My husband George Eltman, who still lights my fire. Clara Eltman, an endless source of sass and inspiration. The women I'm lucky enough to call family — Jodi Fleishman; Gert Eltman; Harriet, Lynn, and Amy Chawtsky; Lois Reemer; Shirley and Susan Alberstat; and Wini Rush — and my goddaughter, the six-year-old culinary whiz, Ellis Stemple.

To the best girfriends in the world: Patricia Allison, Gloria Epstein, Ann Wall Frank, Lisa Shara Hall, Mittie Hellmich, Amy Godine, Shirley Kishiyama, Suzy Kitman, Trink Morimitsu, Josie Mosley, Ronni Olitsky, Susan Orlean, Sara Perry, Miriam Seger, Joan Strouse.

To Victoria Frey, the wonder woman and extraordinary cook; and Peter and Julian Leitner, who own a piece of soul.

To Tim Sills: Forever, my word mate.

And to the loving memory of my father, Alan H. Fleishman.

DIANE MORGAN THANKS:
My husband Greg Morgan, love and soul mate for life; and my children Eric and Molly, my favorite recipe tasters and critics extraordinaire.

To my best girfriends, I'll go with you for a latte or Cosmopolitan any time: Harriet Watson, Margie Sanders, Marci Taylor, Cam Kimball, Priscilla Longfield, Laurie Turney, Cheryl Russell, Margarita Leon, Mary Corpening Barber, Sara Corpening Whiteford, Katherine Alford, Toni Allegra, Heidi Yorkshire, Summer Jameson, Josie Jimenez, Melinda Gable, and Debbie Adams.

REED DARMON THANKS:
Mittie Hellmich for her fine photos, Ann Hughes for use of her stunning apron collection, and Azi Rad at Chronicle for her sharp eye. Cheers also to Pammela, Kalim, Moto, William, Lisa, and Jack the BBQ genius.